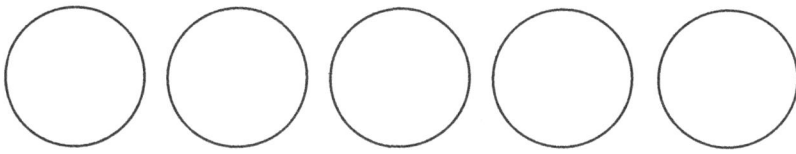

Grab your Dot Markers and get ready for 50 pages of vehicle fun!

Trucks, Trains, Planes, Space, Diggers, Rescue and more...all with big, easy to fill dots, designed to be compatible with all leading dot marker brands with consistent 0.75 inch (18mm) dots.

Ideally suited for kids ages 1-4 as they discover the world around them. This book is intended to boost your child's early development with engaging designs that build connections with words, pictures and colors. All the original artwork has been created by experienced designers to be the right level for kids to stimulate their imagination, to allow them to build their fine motor skills and to have a load of fun and learning in the process!

We know how enthusiastic little dot marker artists can be, so we've kept our designs on one side of the paper only to reduce the chance of colors bleeding through. As parents, we also know that adding an extra piece of paper or card between pages is also a great idea!

Thank you for purchasing this book and we hope you and your little ones unlock a world of dot marker fun and learning! We're still learning and growing ourselves, so we'd really appreciate a review on Amazon for this book if you have time.
Thank you.

Loads more from Under The Cover Press
available at amazon

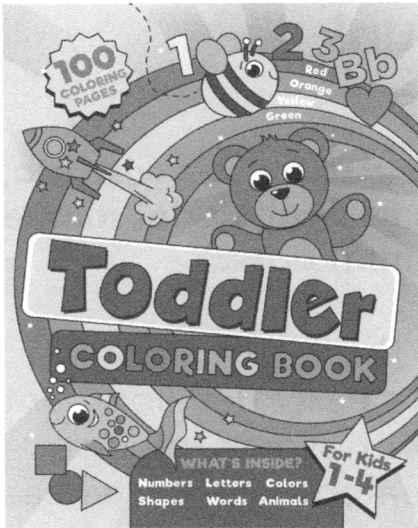

ISBN 979-8552067565

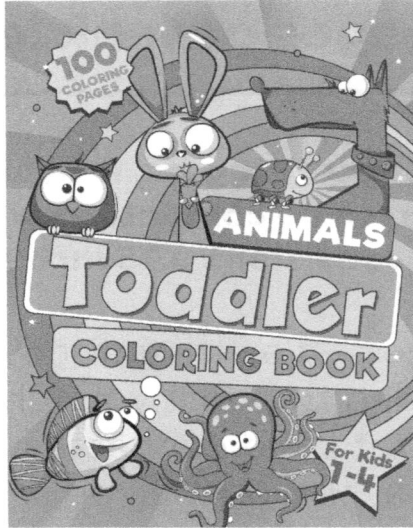

ISBN 979-8509492808

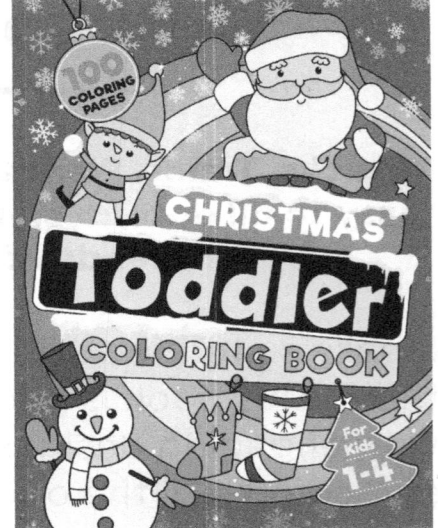

ISBN 979-8473139457

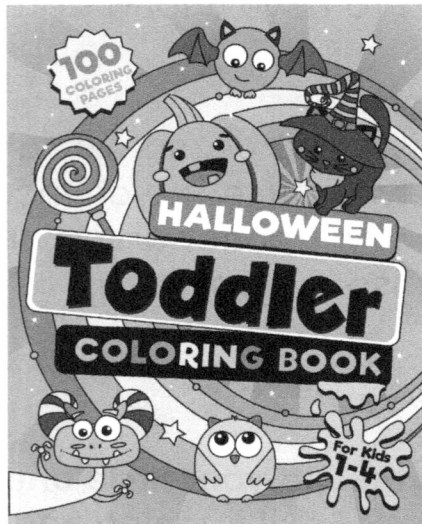

ISBN 979-8548451484

ISBN 979-8590346219

ISBN 979-8520557715

ISBN 979-8559845876

ISBN 979-8559850436

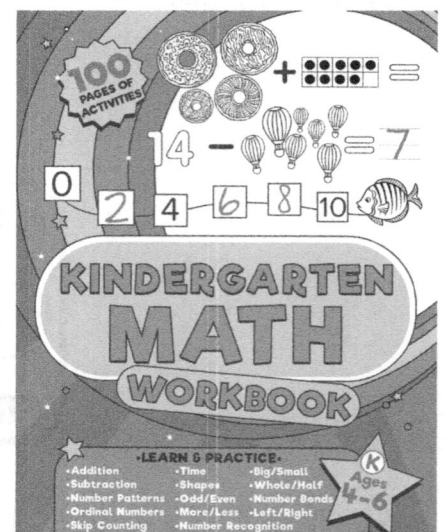

ISBN 979-8717778565

This Vehicles Dot Markers Activity Book

BELONGS TO...

....

USE YOUR MARKERS TO FILL ALL THE DOTS!

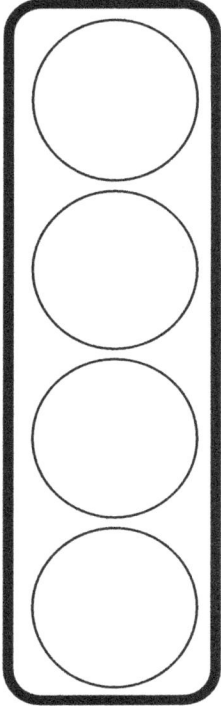

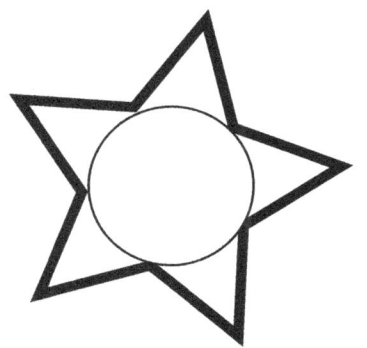

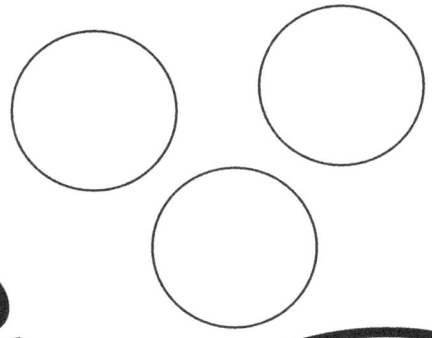

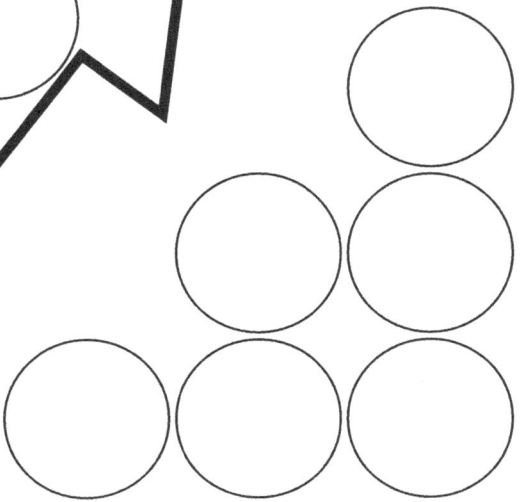

TIME FOR A PRACTICE!

BULLDOZER

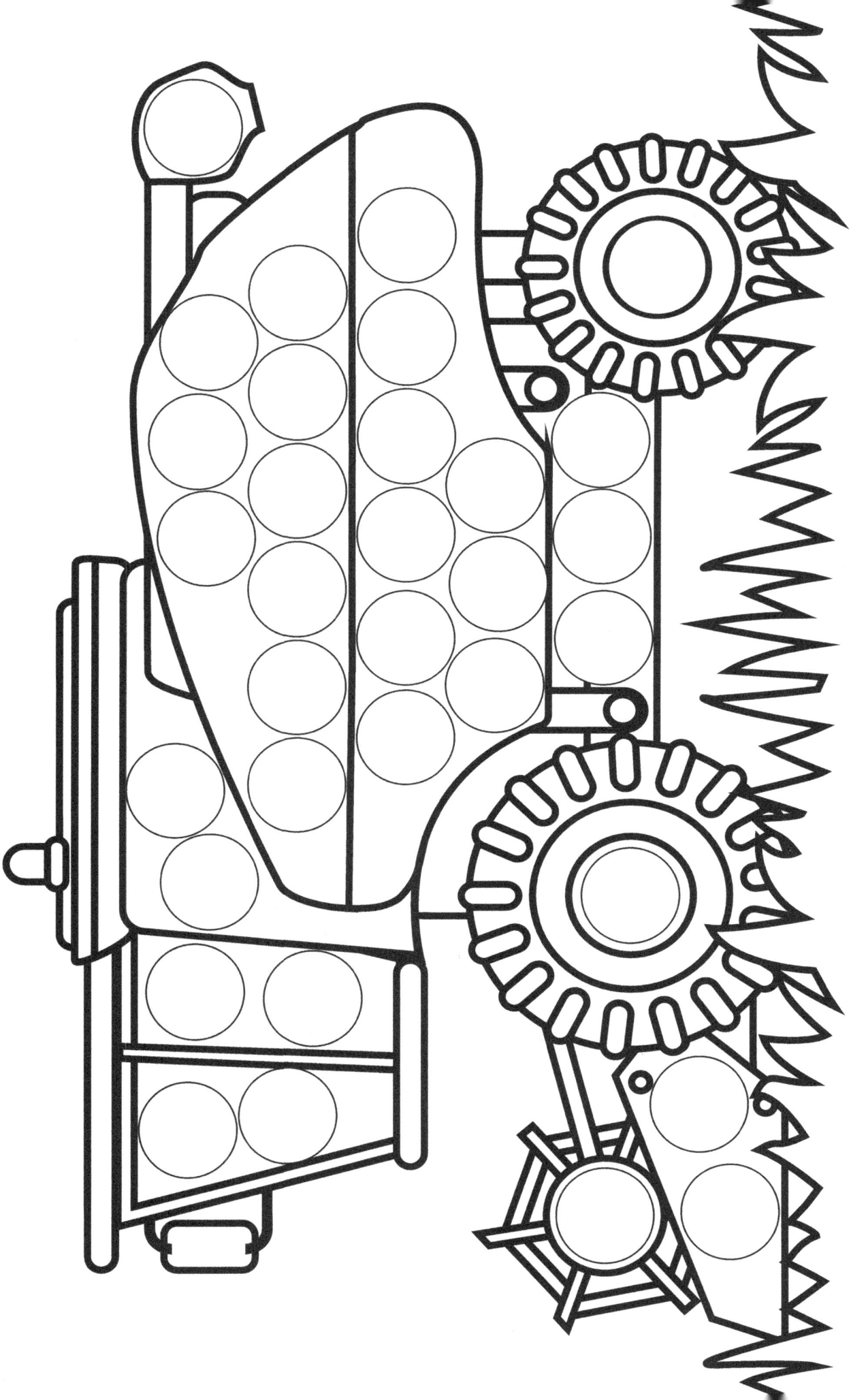

COMBINE HARVESTER

SPEEDY!

3

DUNE BUGGY

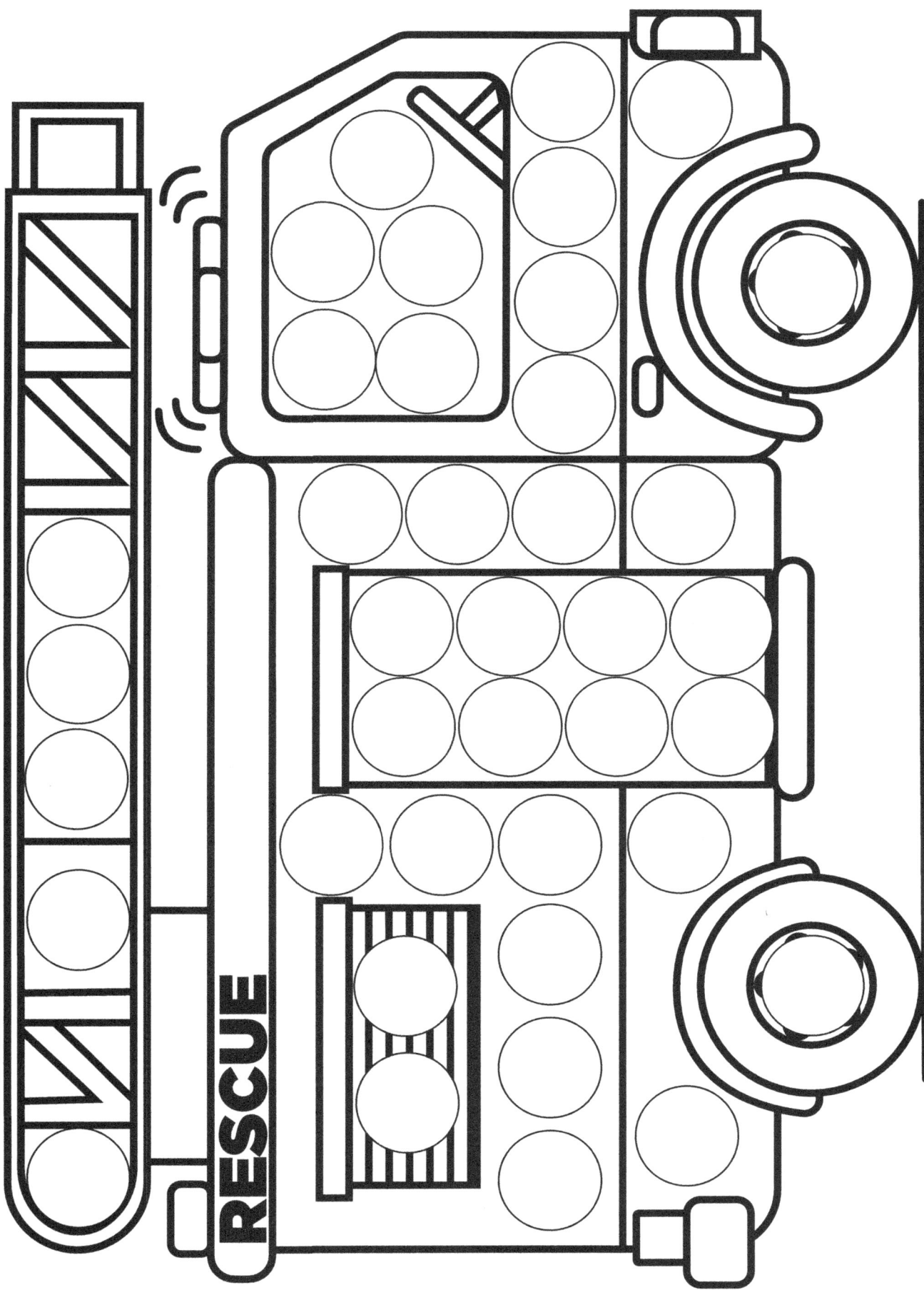

RESCUE

FIRE TRUCK

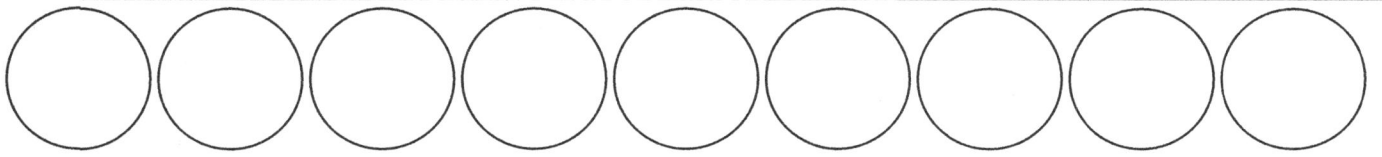

FORKLIFT TRUCK

GALLEON

ICE CREAM TRUCK

LUNAR LANDER

OCEAN EXPLORER

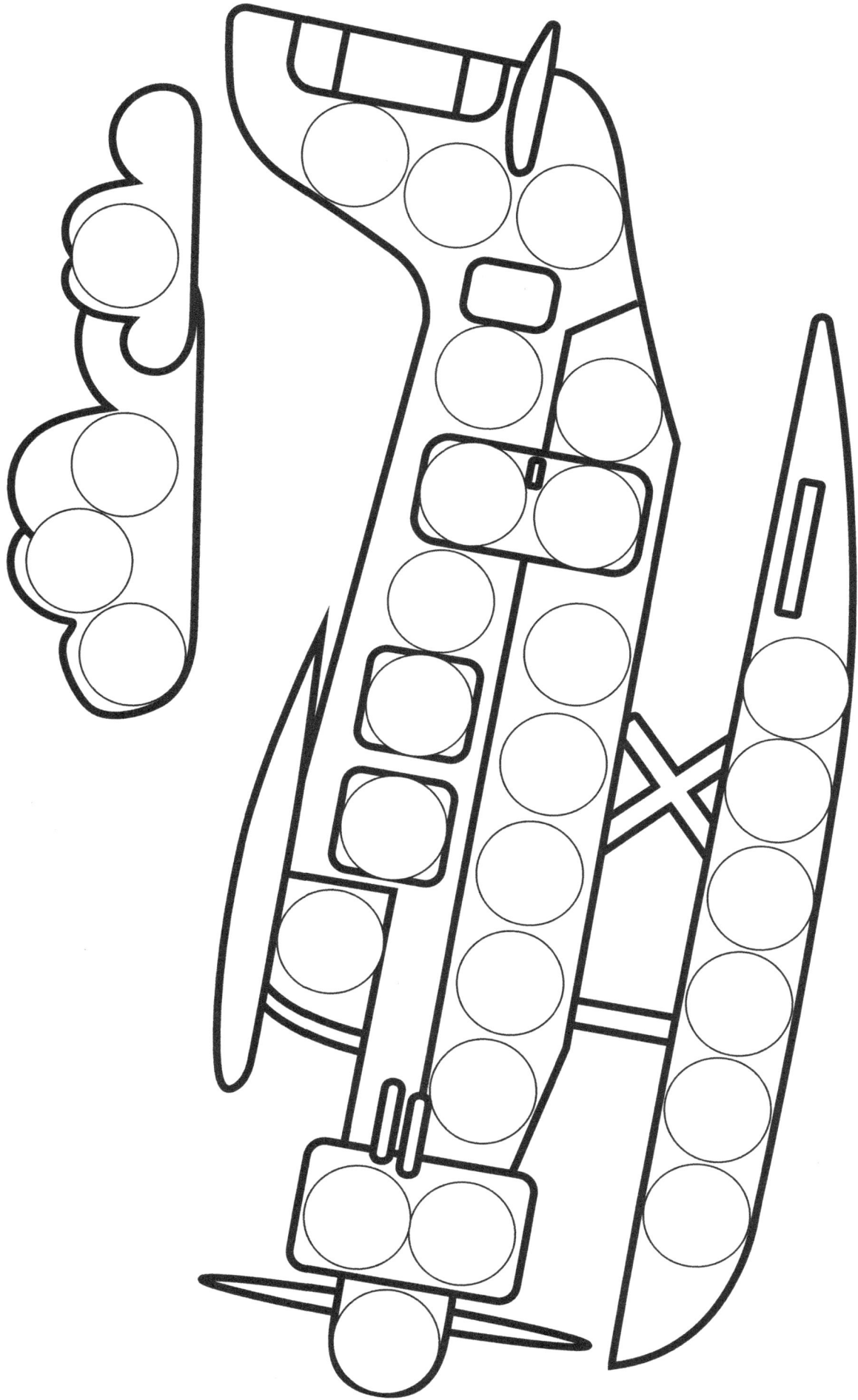

SEAPLANE

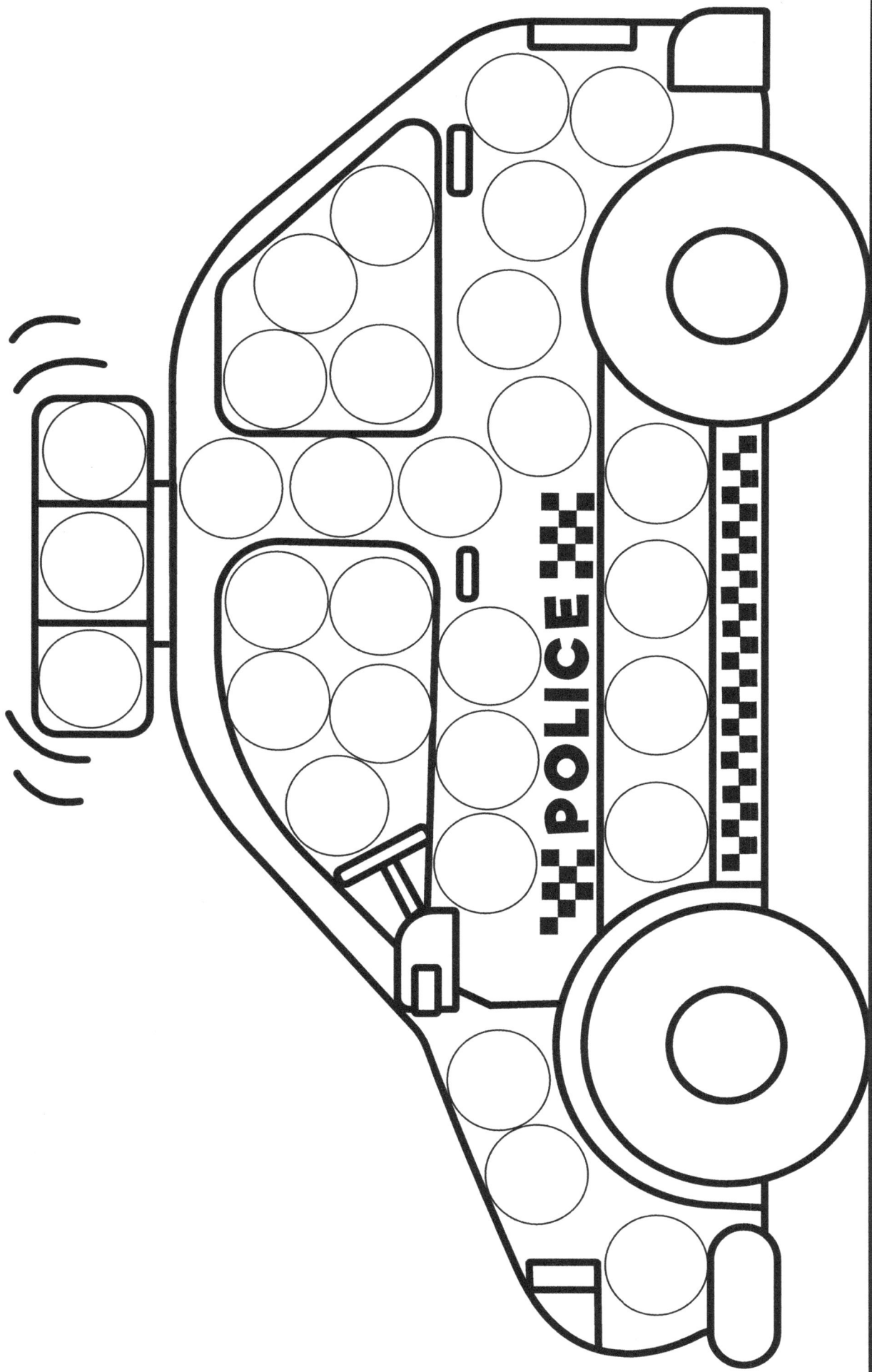

POLICE CAR

POLICE

MONSTER TRUCK

AMBULANCE

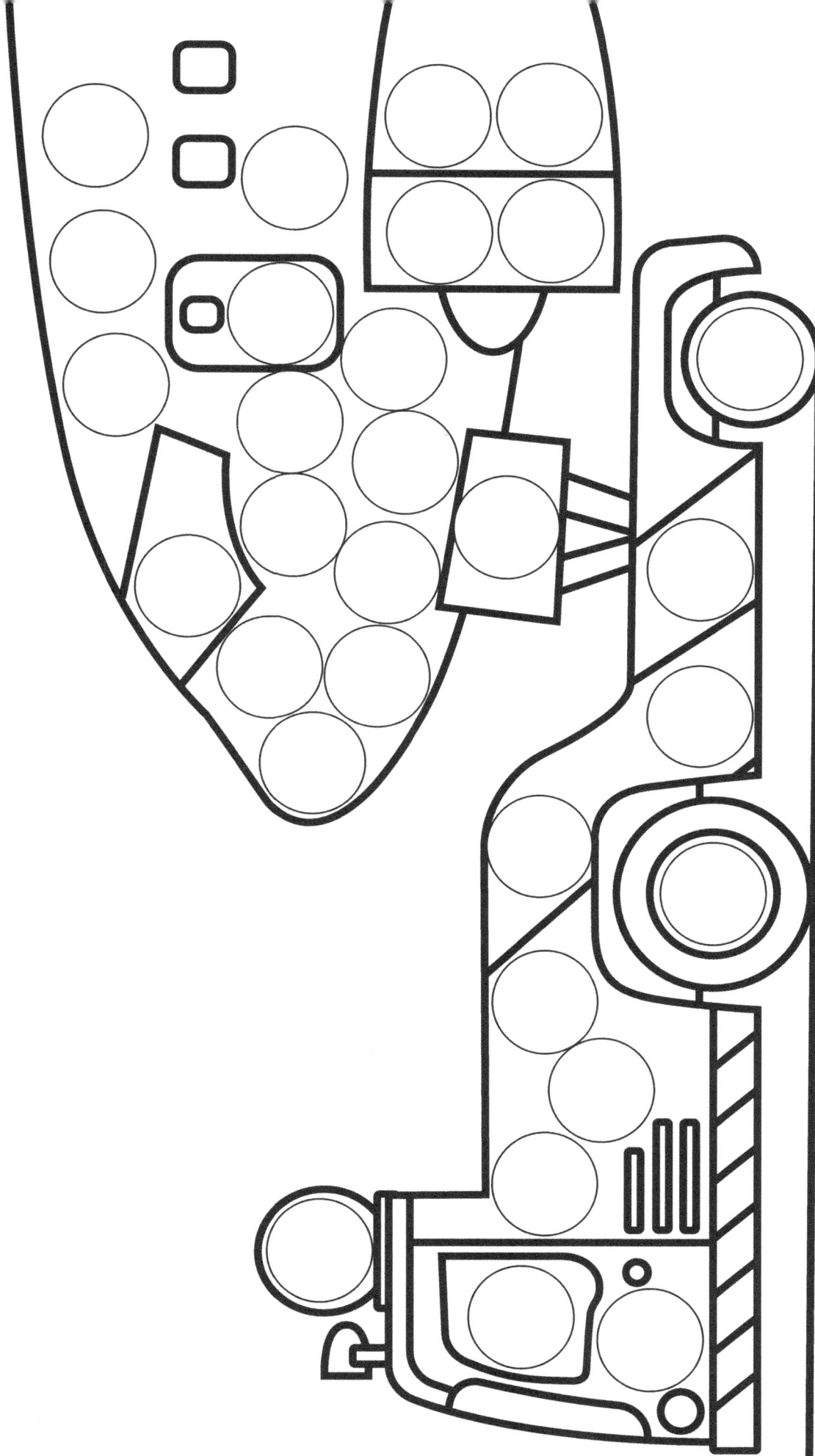

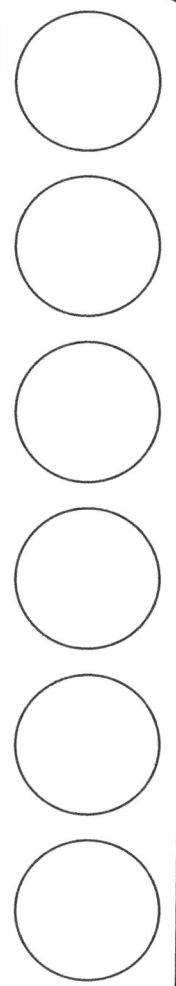

AIRCRAFT TUG

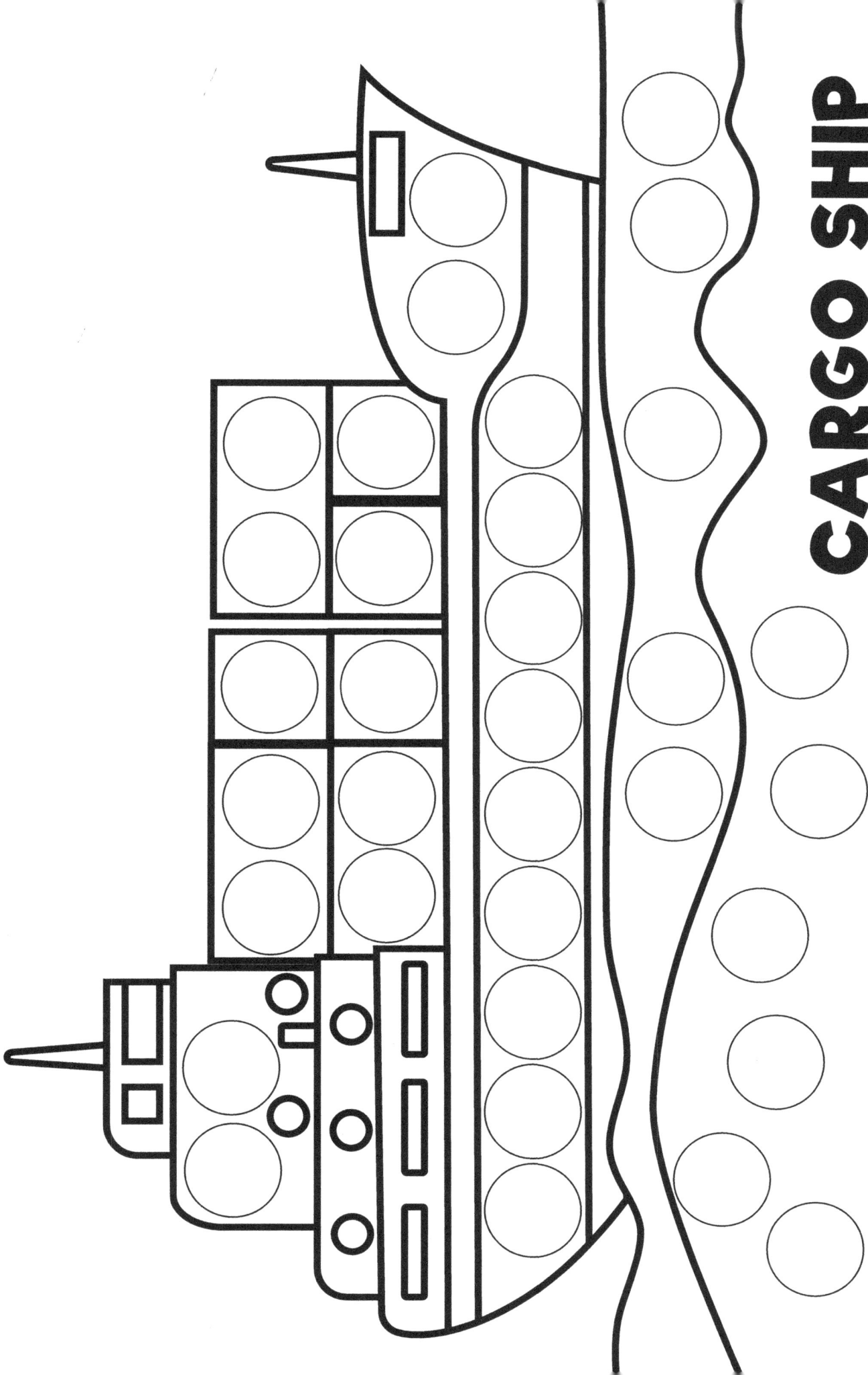

CARGO SHIP

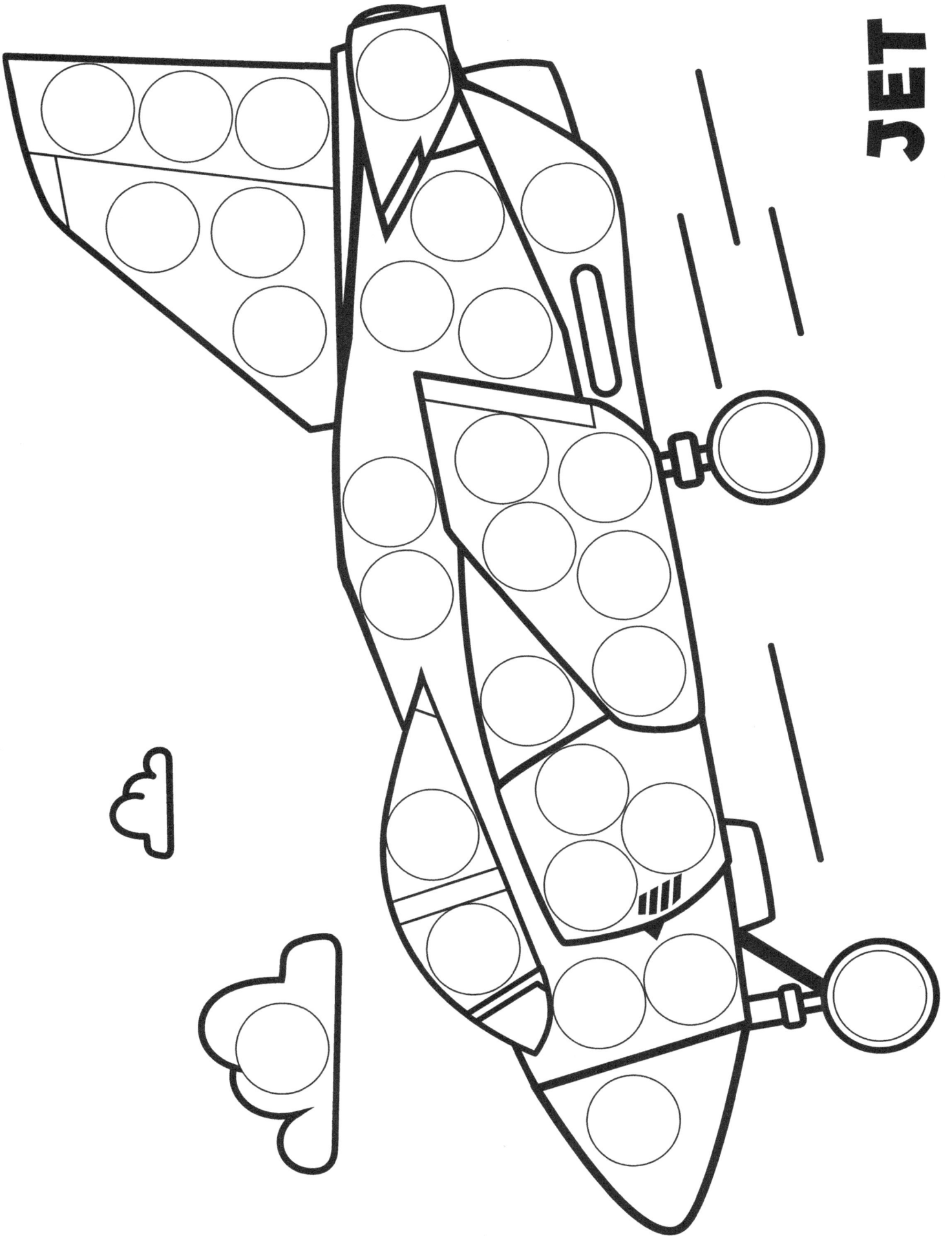

JET

UP...UP...UP!

MOBILE CRANE

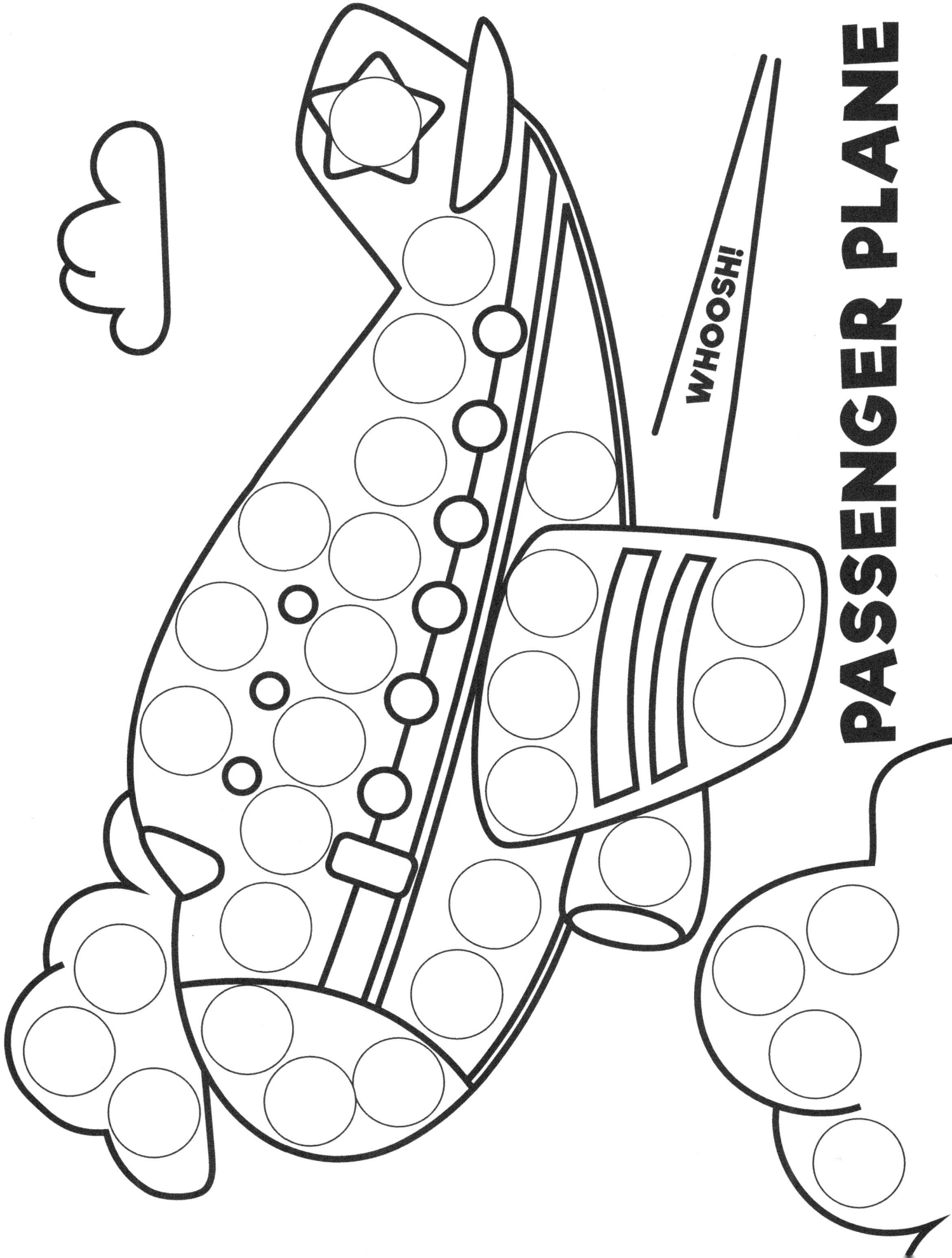

WHOOSH!

PASSENGER PLANE

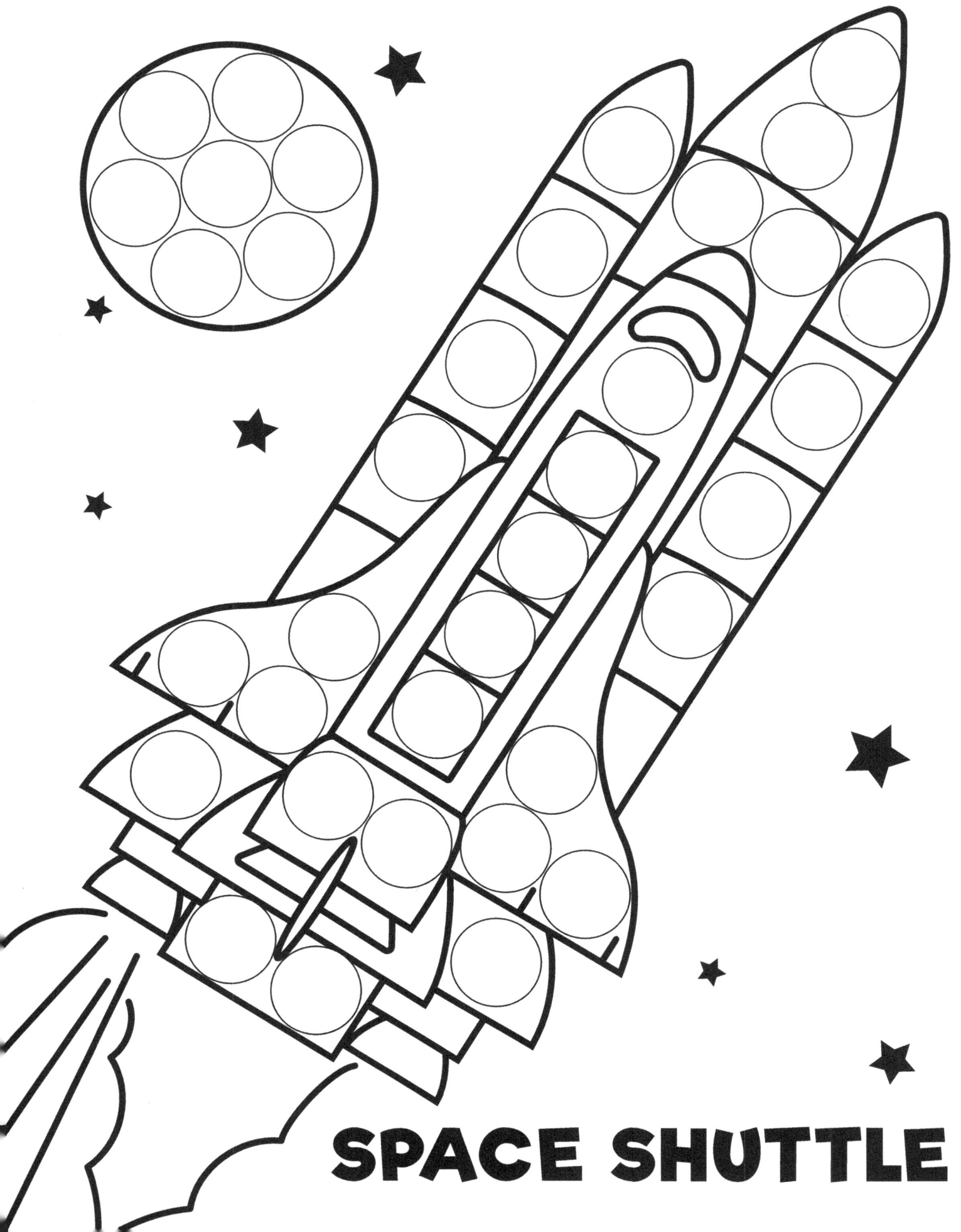

SPACE SHUTTLE

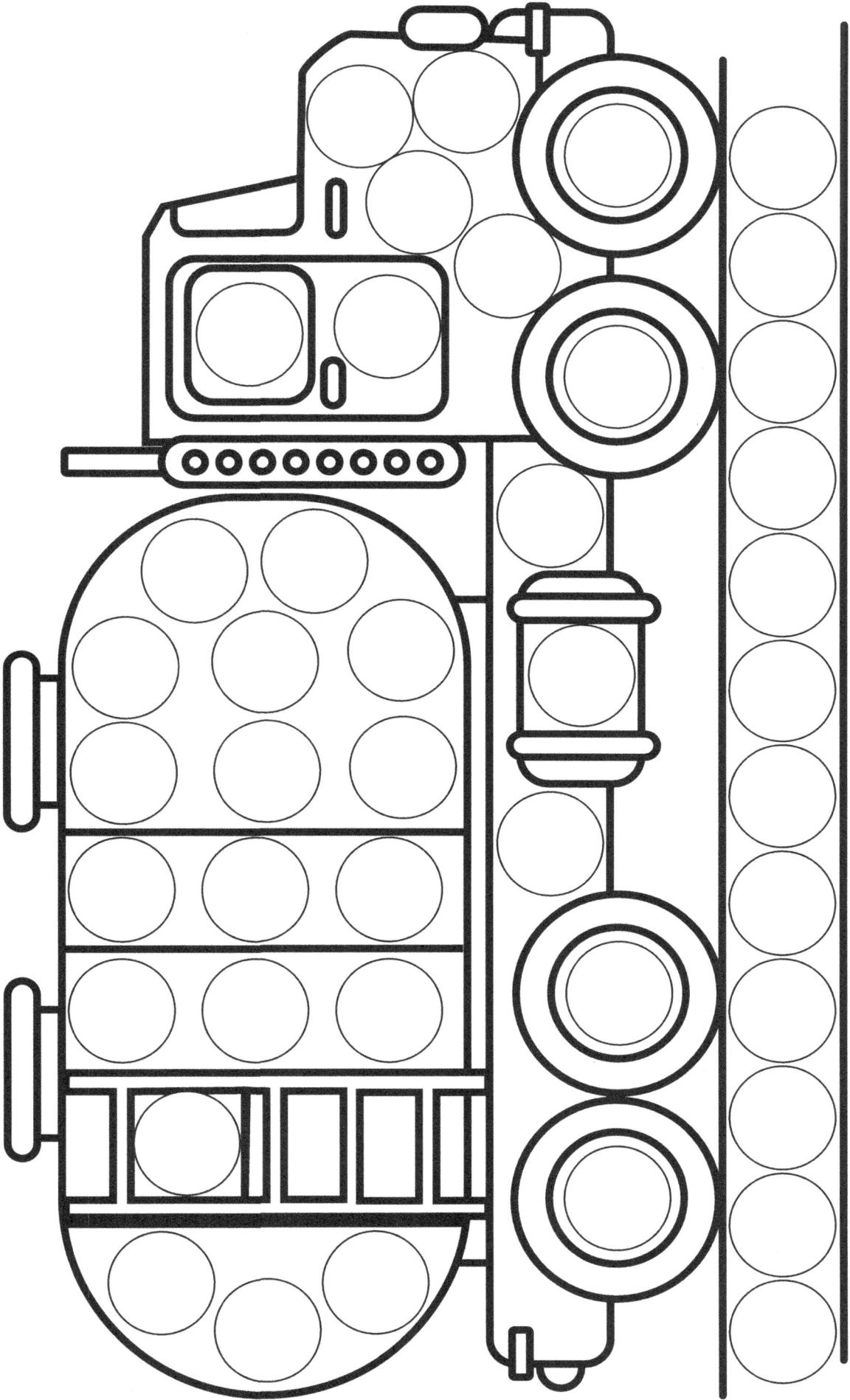

TANKER

UFO

YACHT

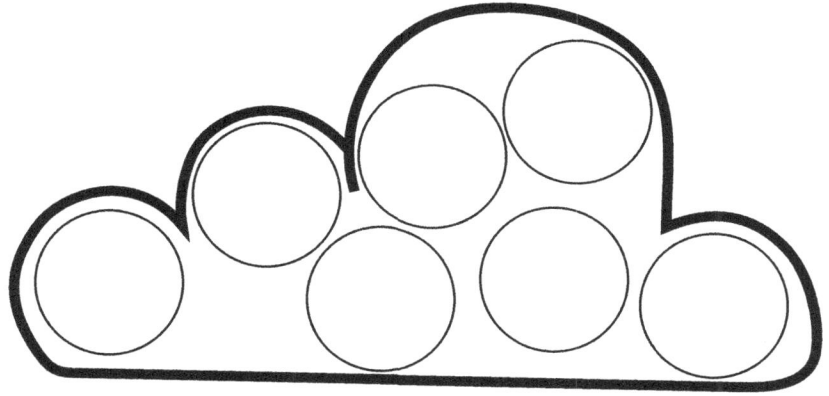

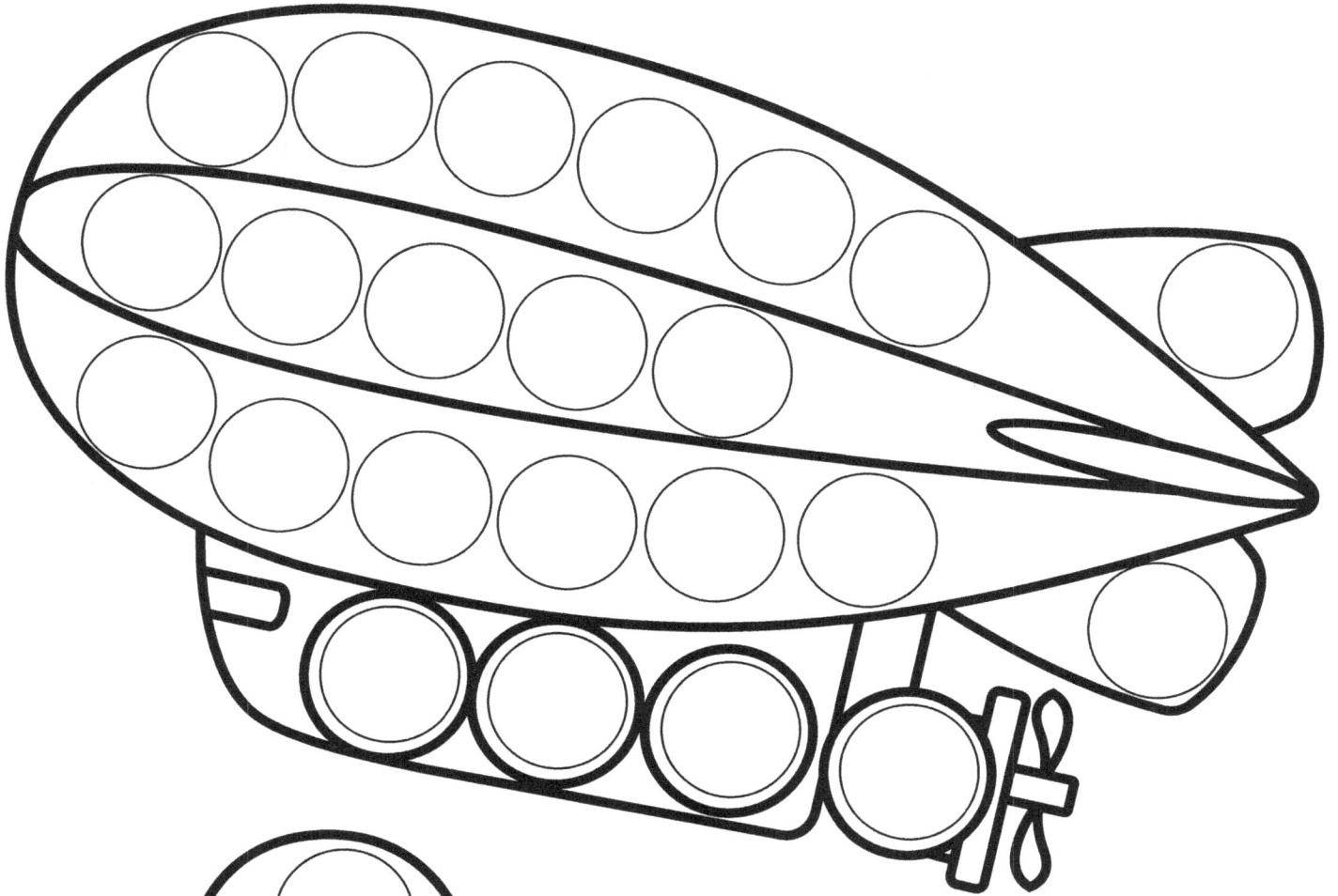

BLIMP

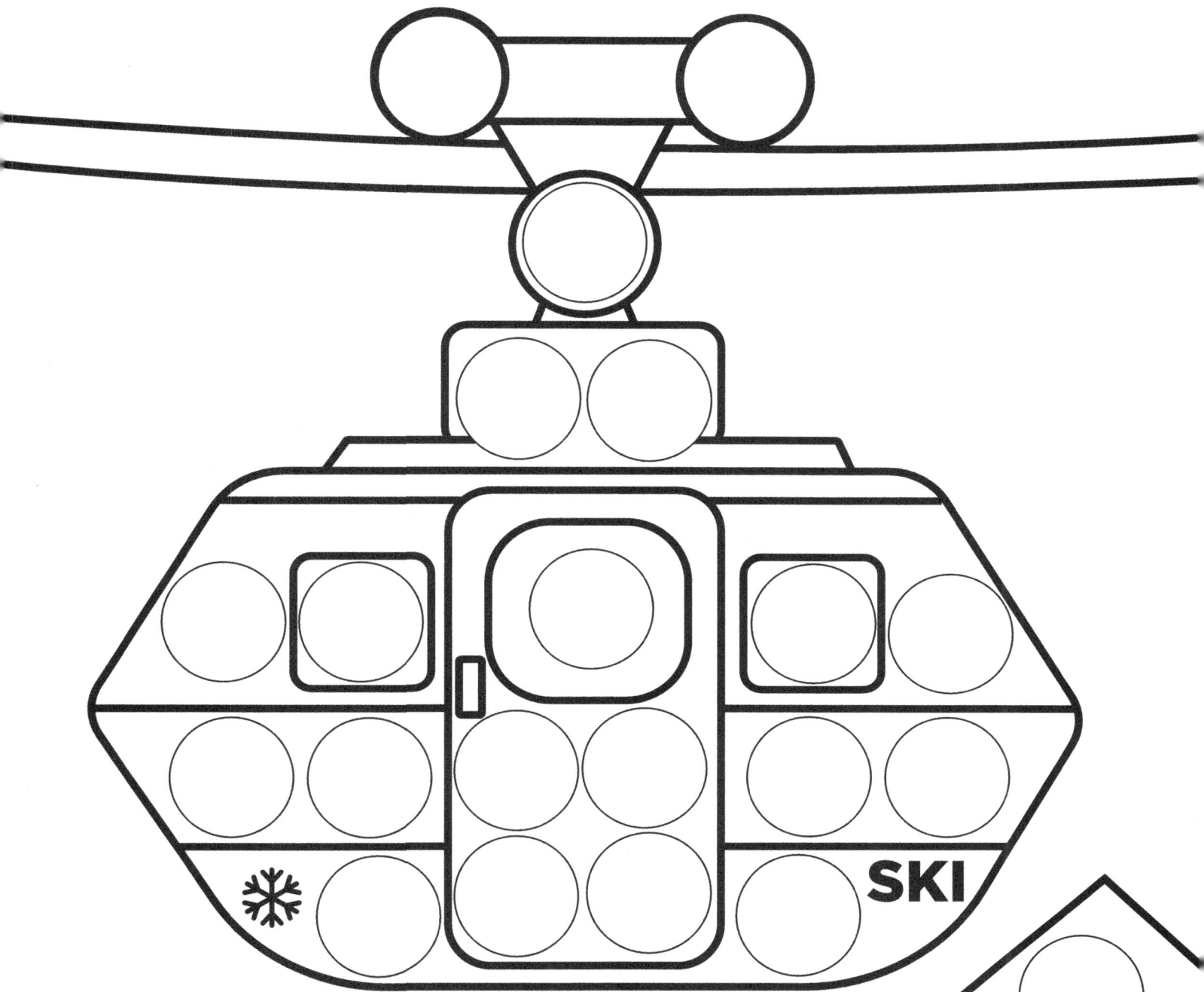

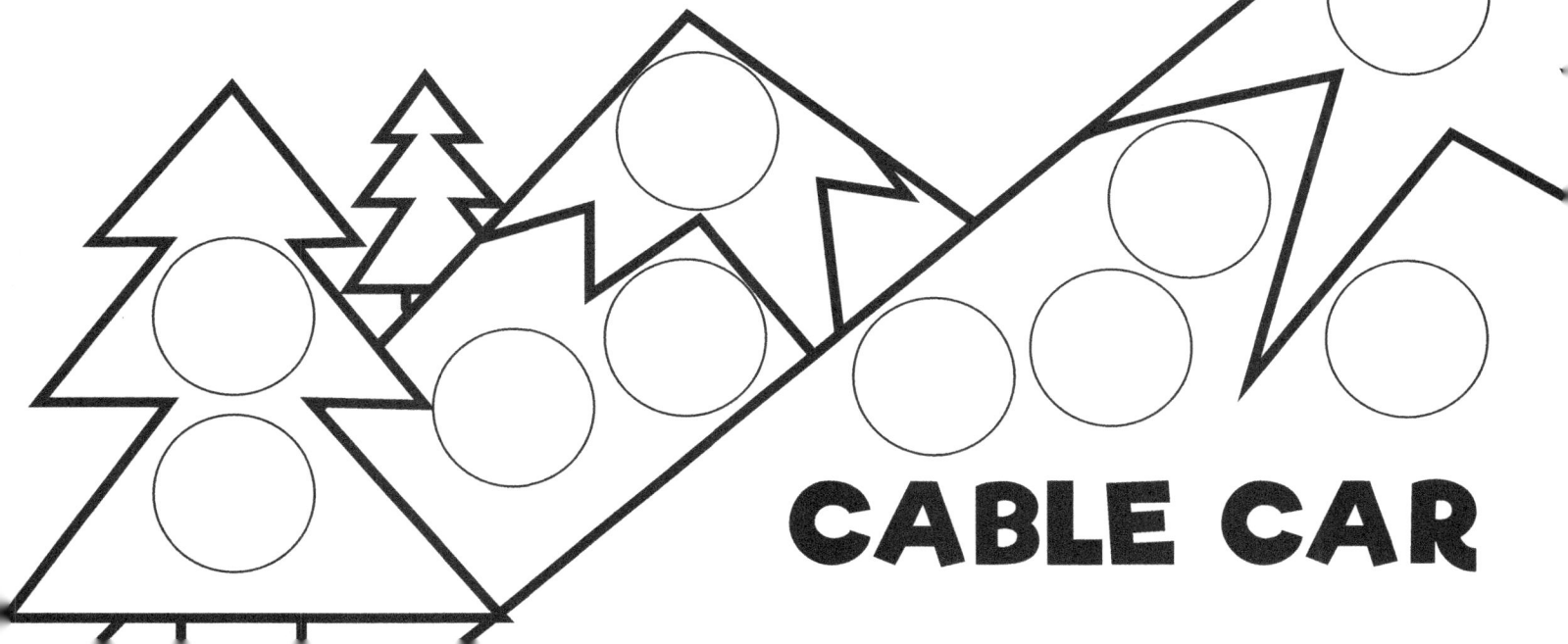

SKI

CABLE CAR

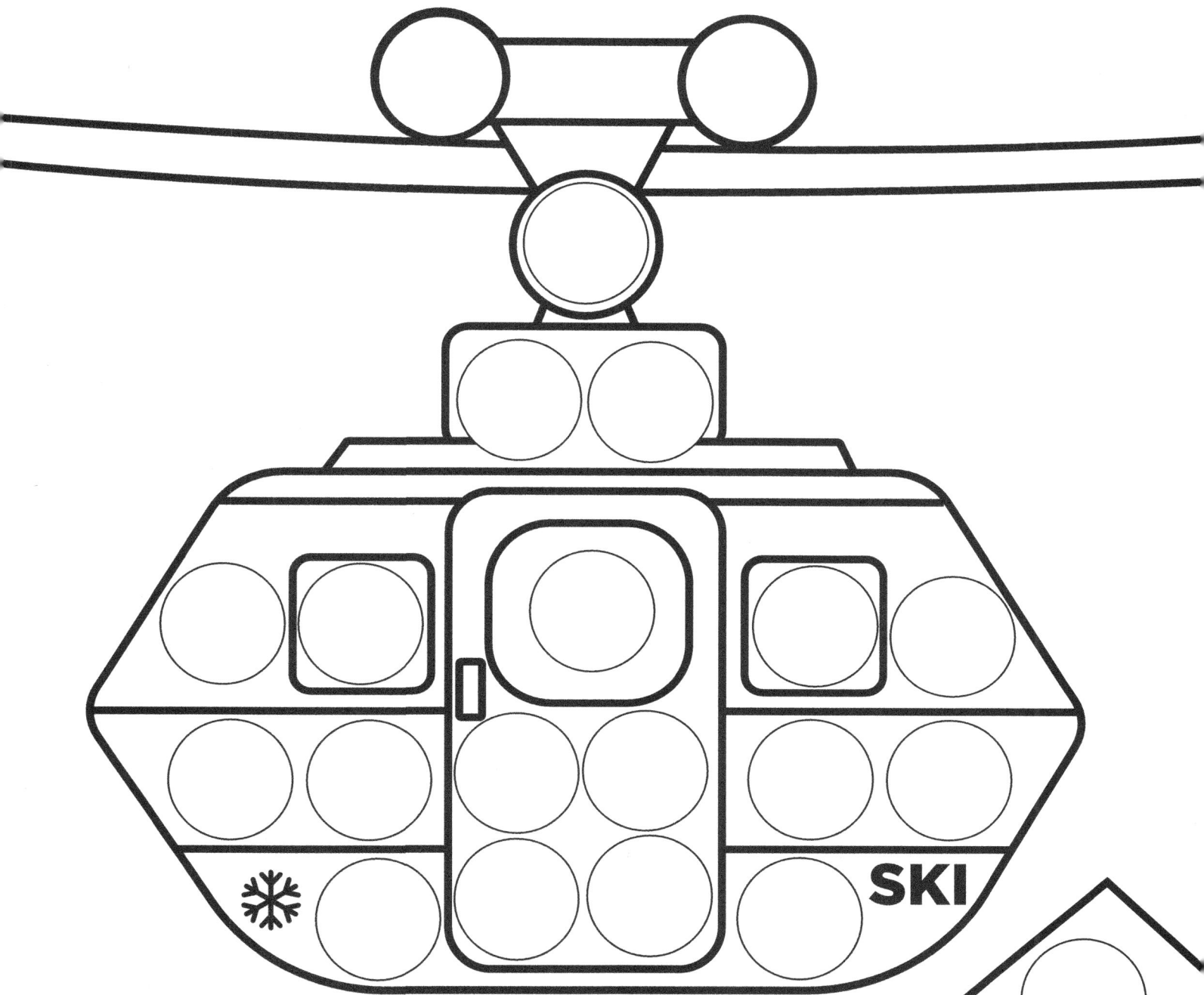

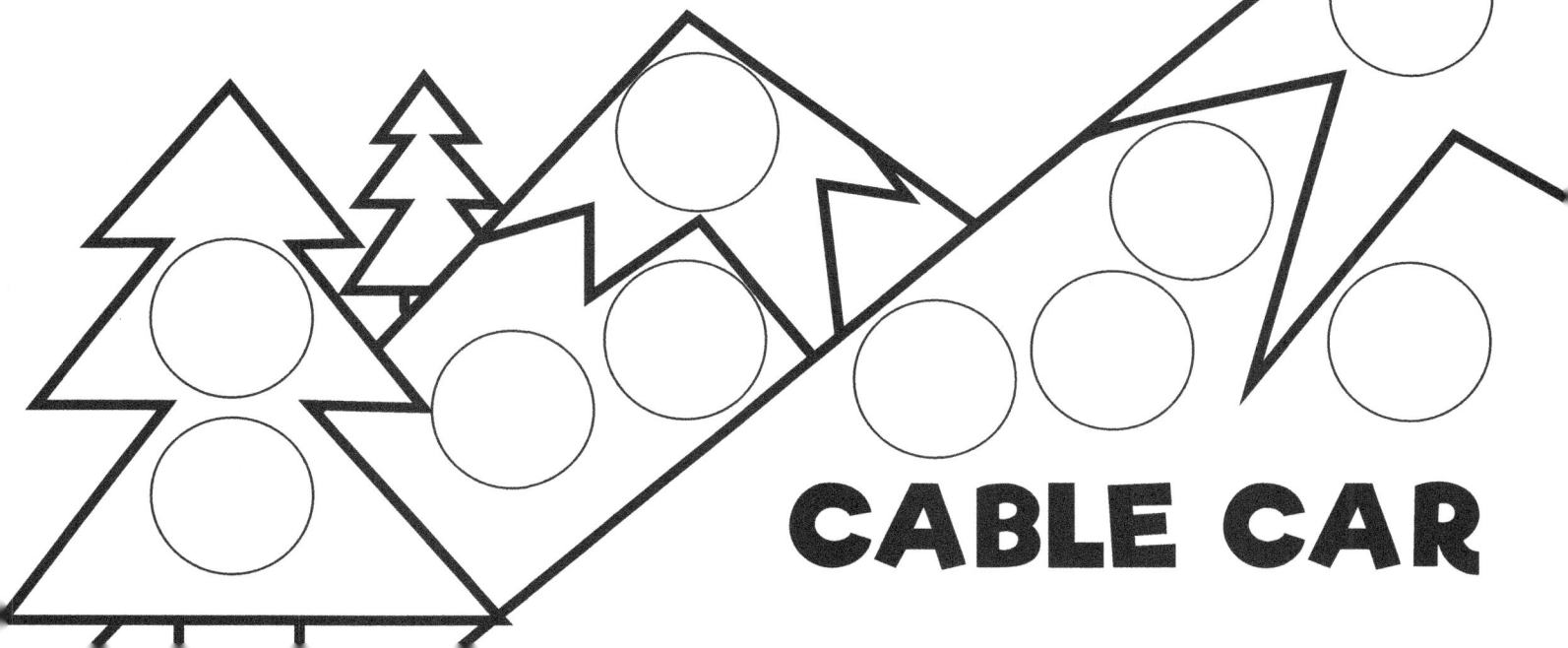

SKI

CABLE CAR

CITY BUS

DEMOLITION CRANE

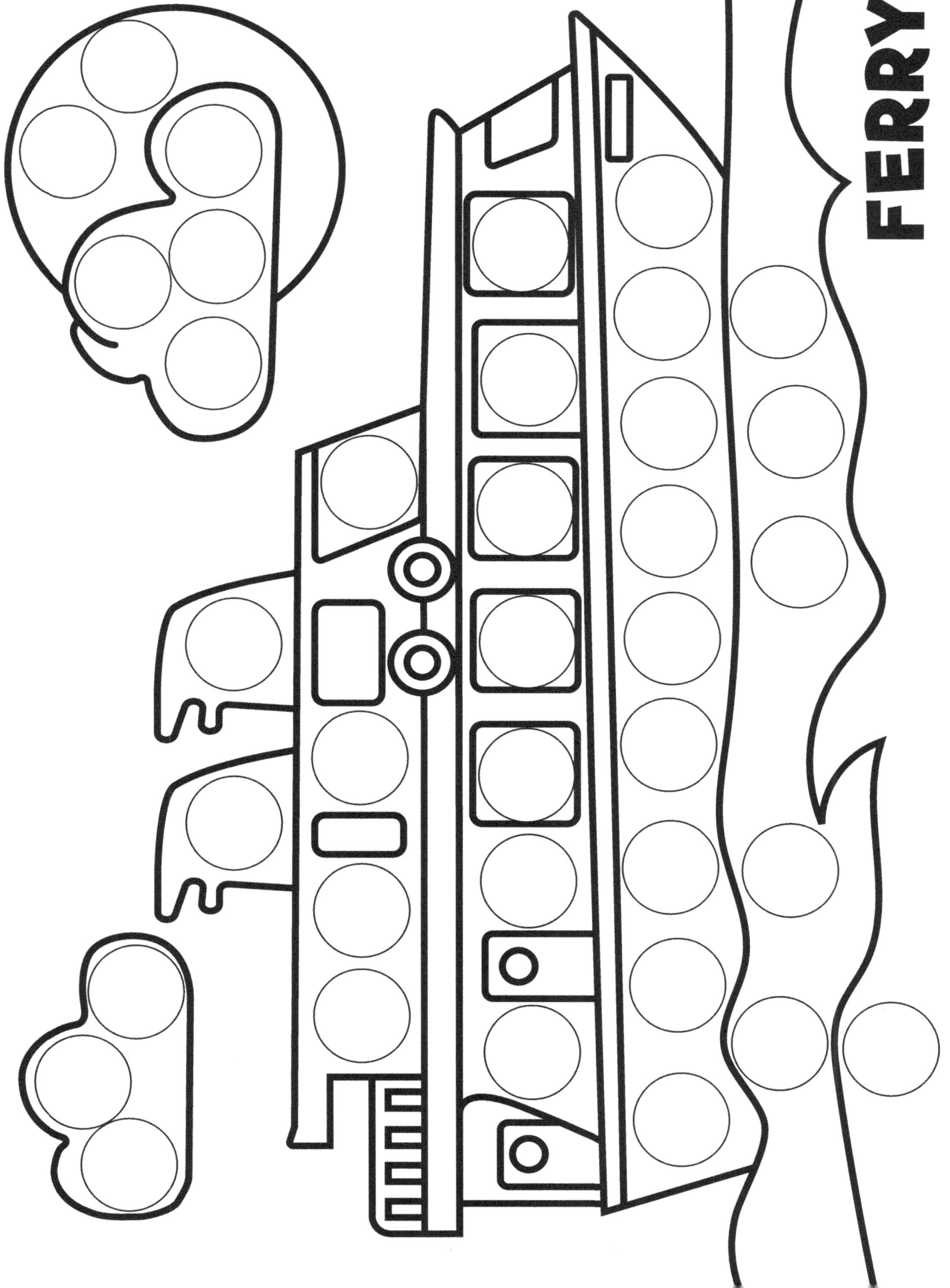

FERRY

CRUNCH!

EXCAVATOR

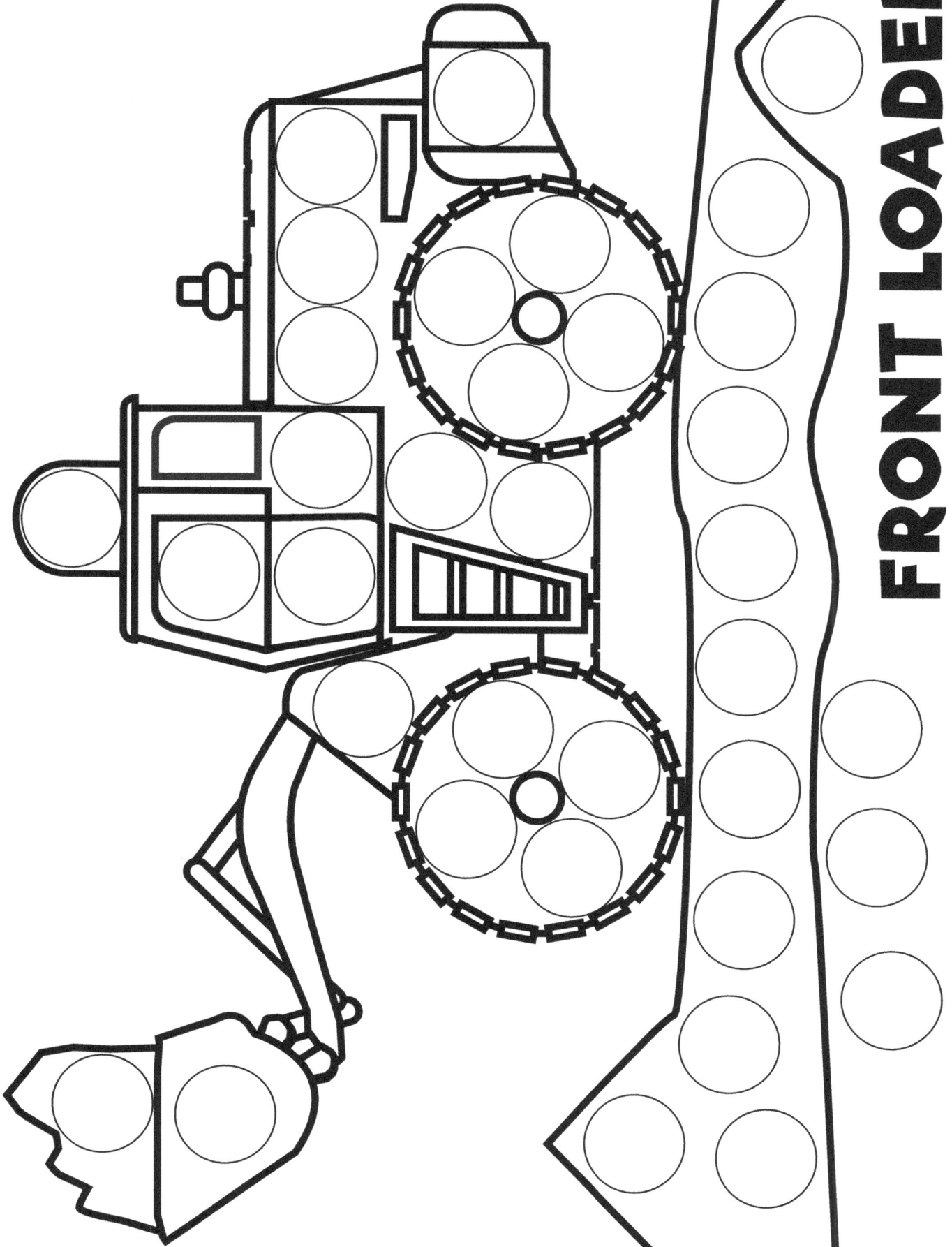

FRONT LOADER

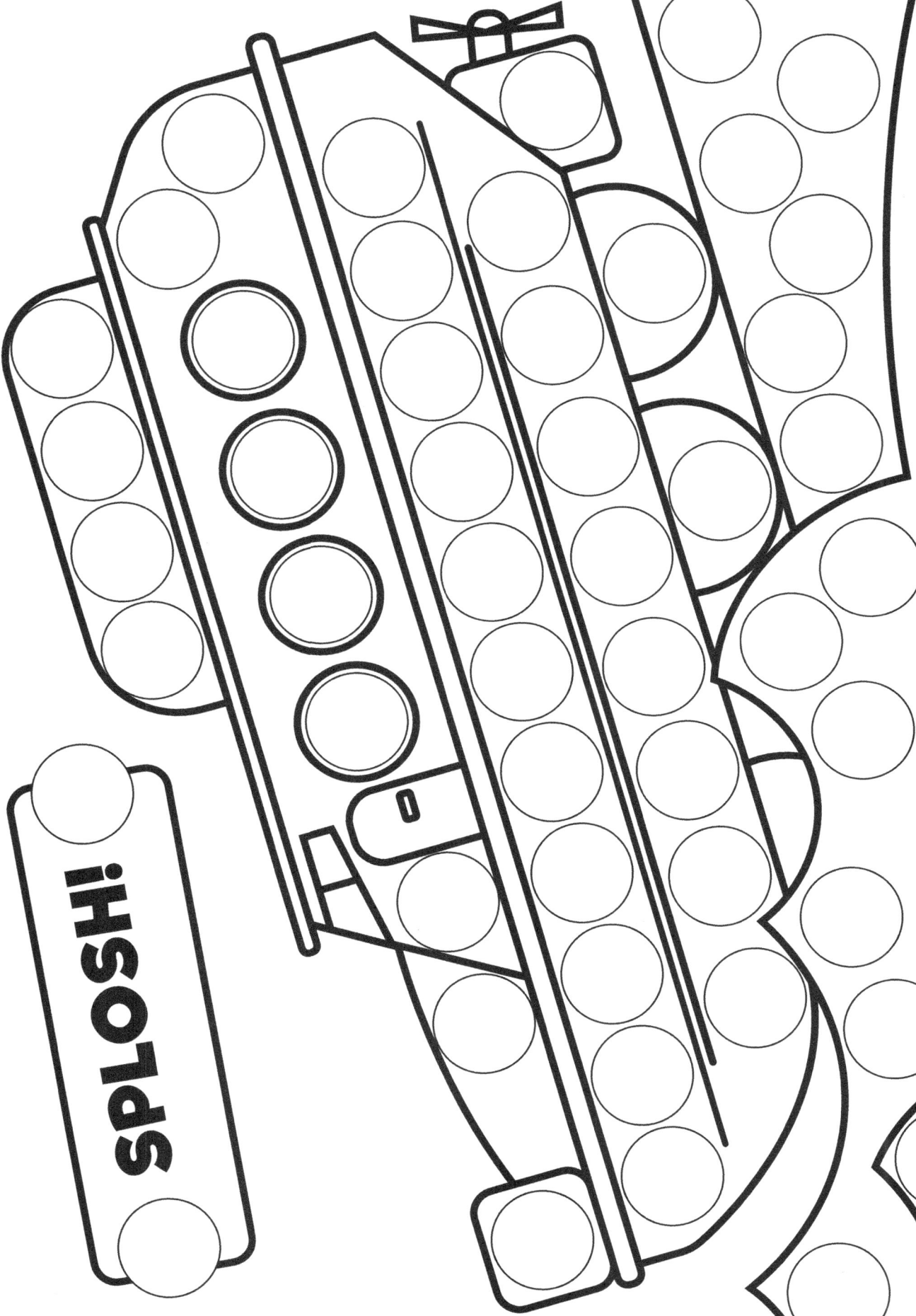

SPLOSH!

AMPHIBIOUS VEHICLE

MINI EXCAVATOR

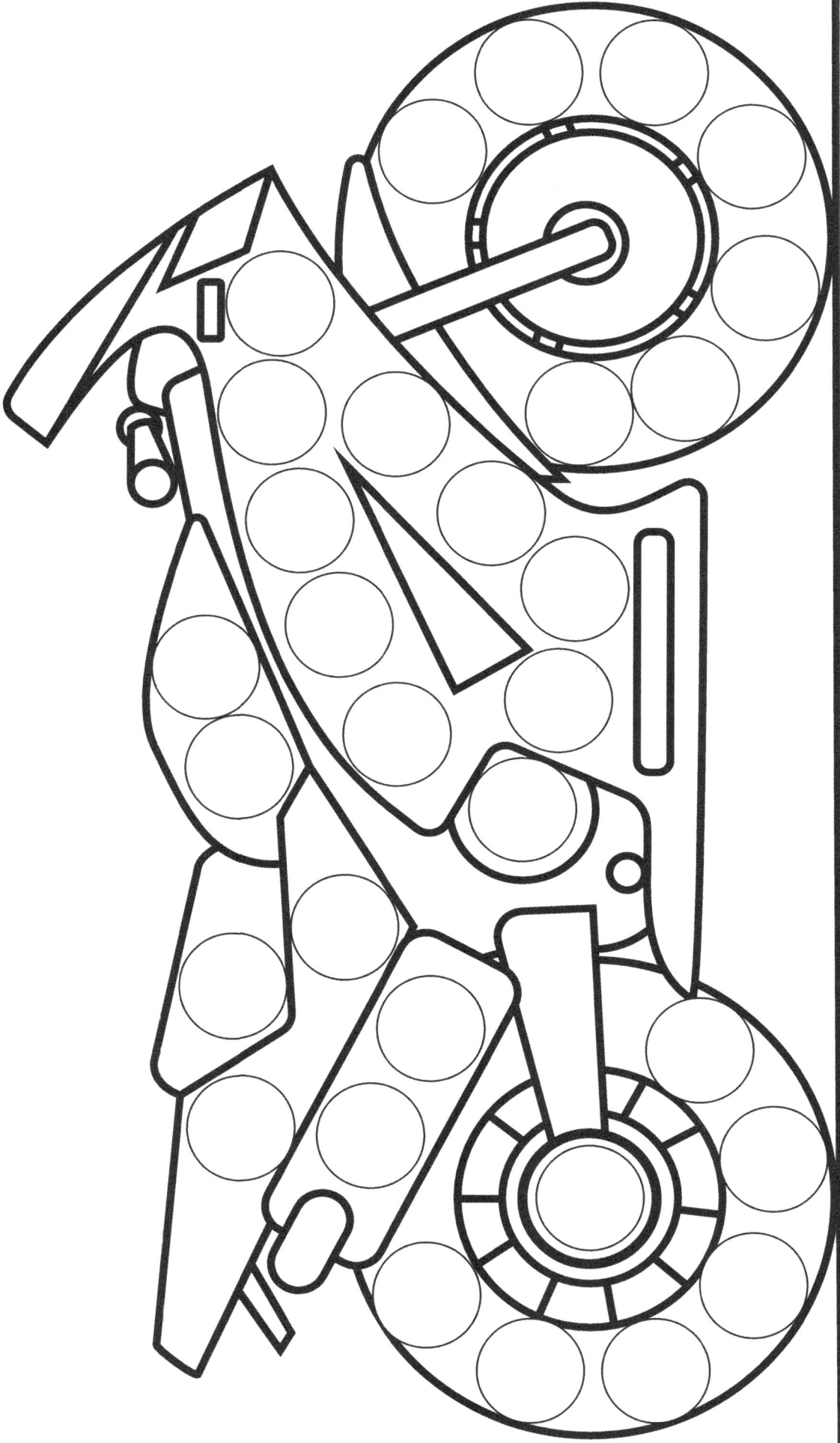

MOTORBIKE

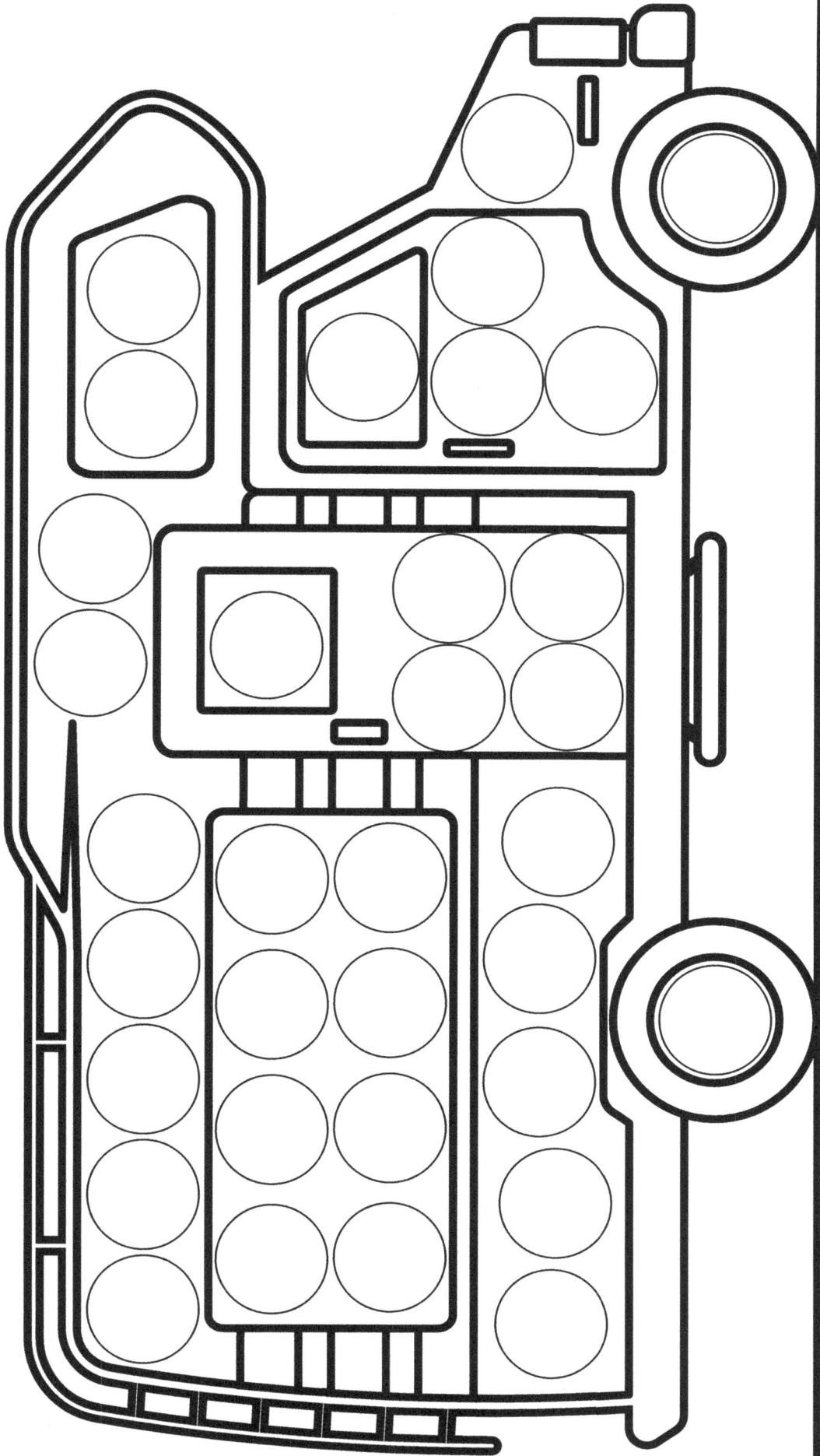
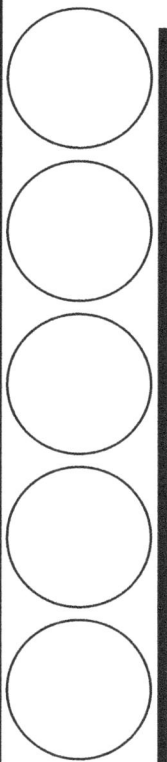

RV MOTORHOME

STEAM TRAIN

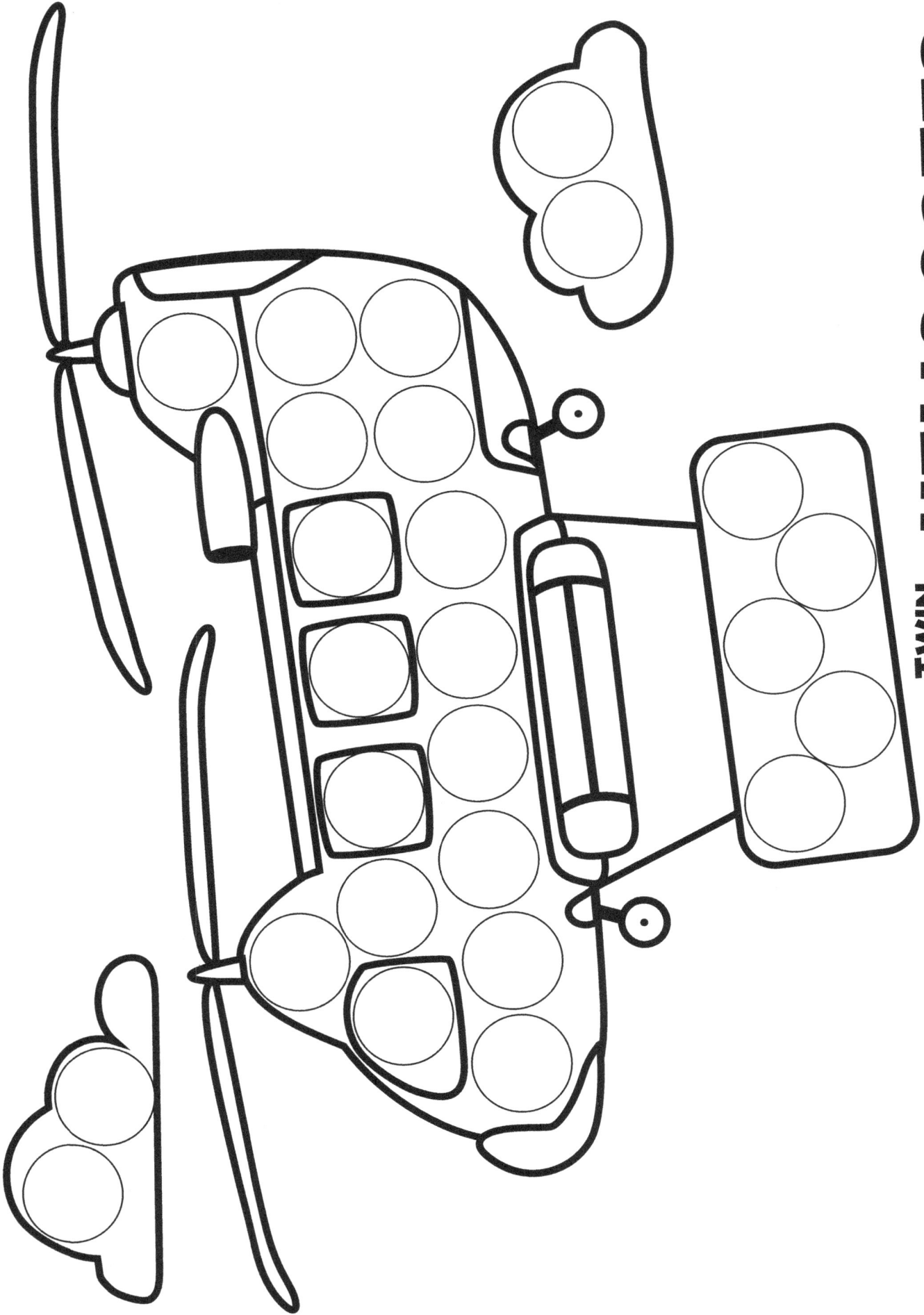

TWIN ROTOR **HELICOPTER**

TWISTING!
TURNING!
MIXING!

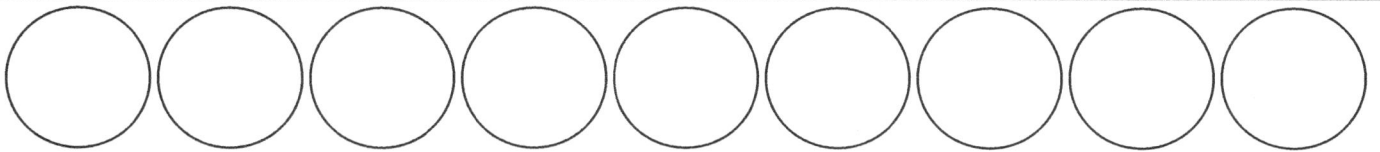

CONCRETE MIXER

HOT AIR BALLOON

POLAR EXPLORER

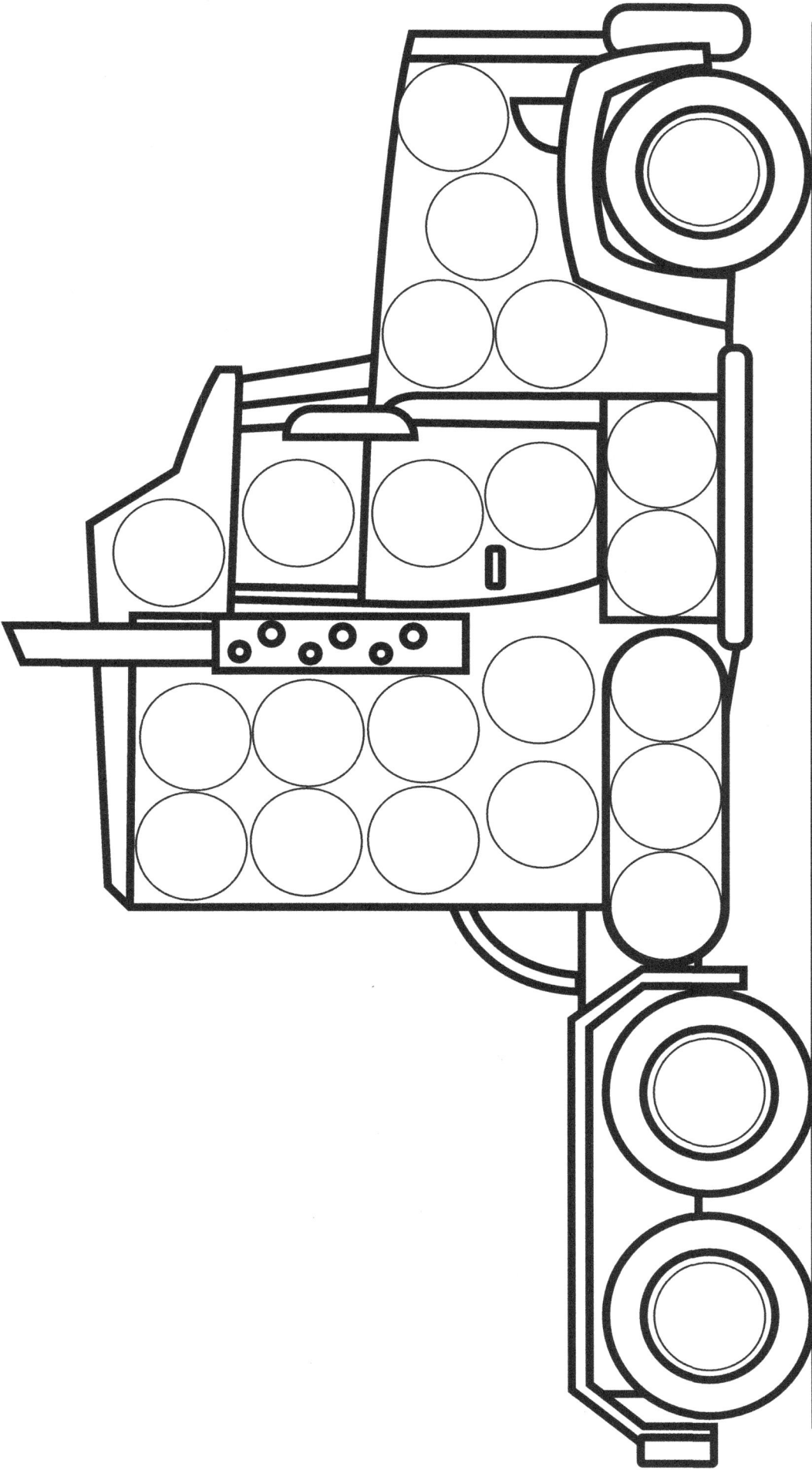

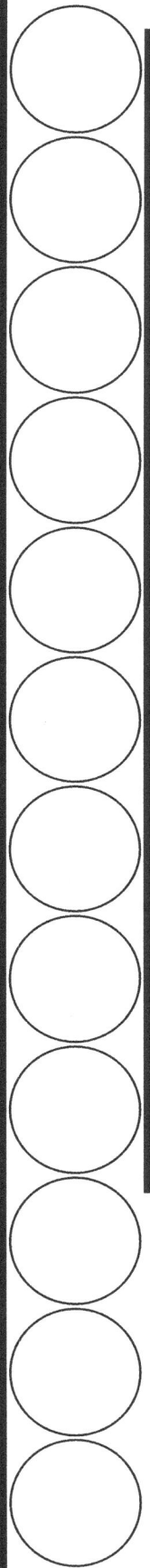

TRUCK

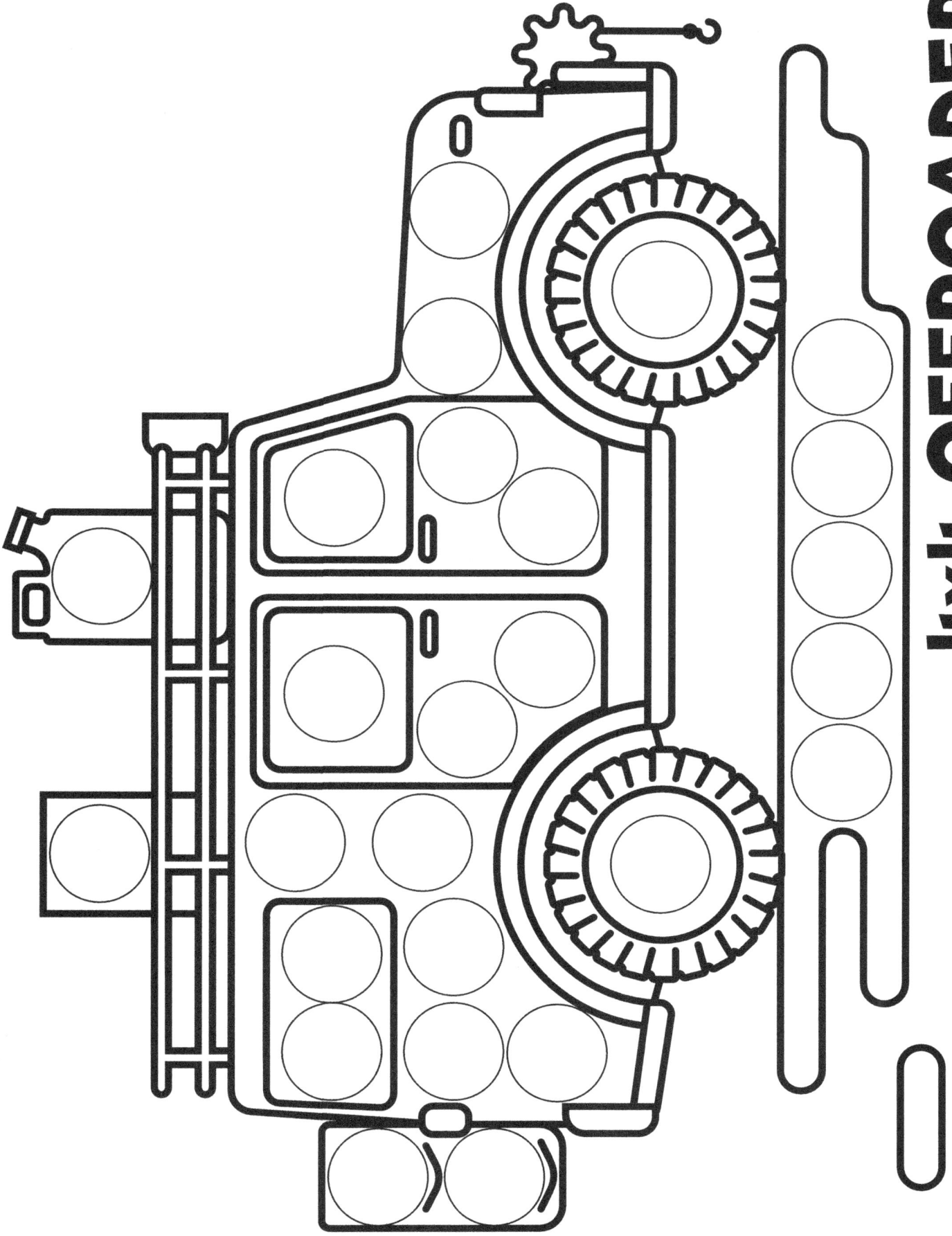

4X4 OFFROADER

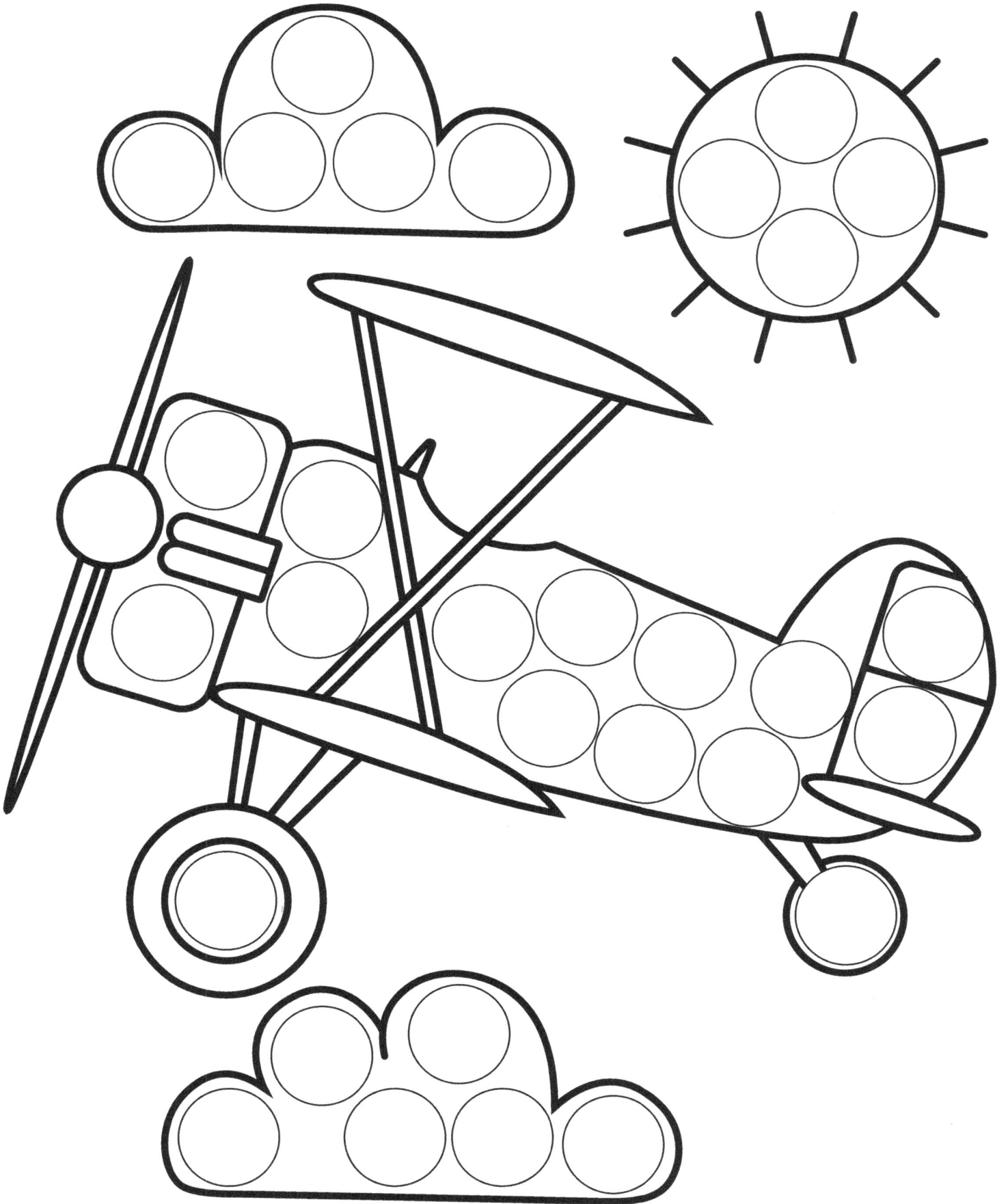

AIRPLANE

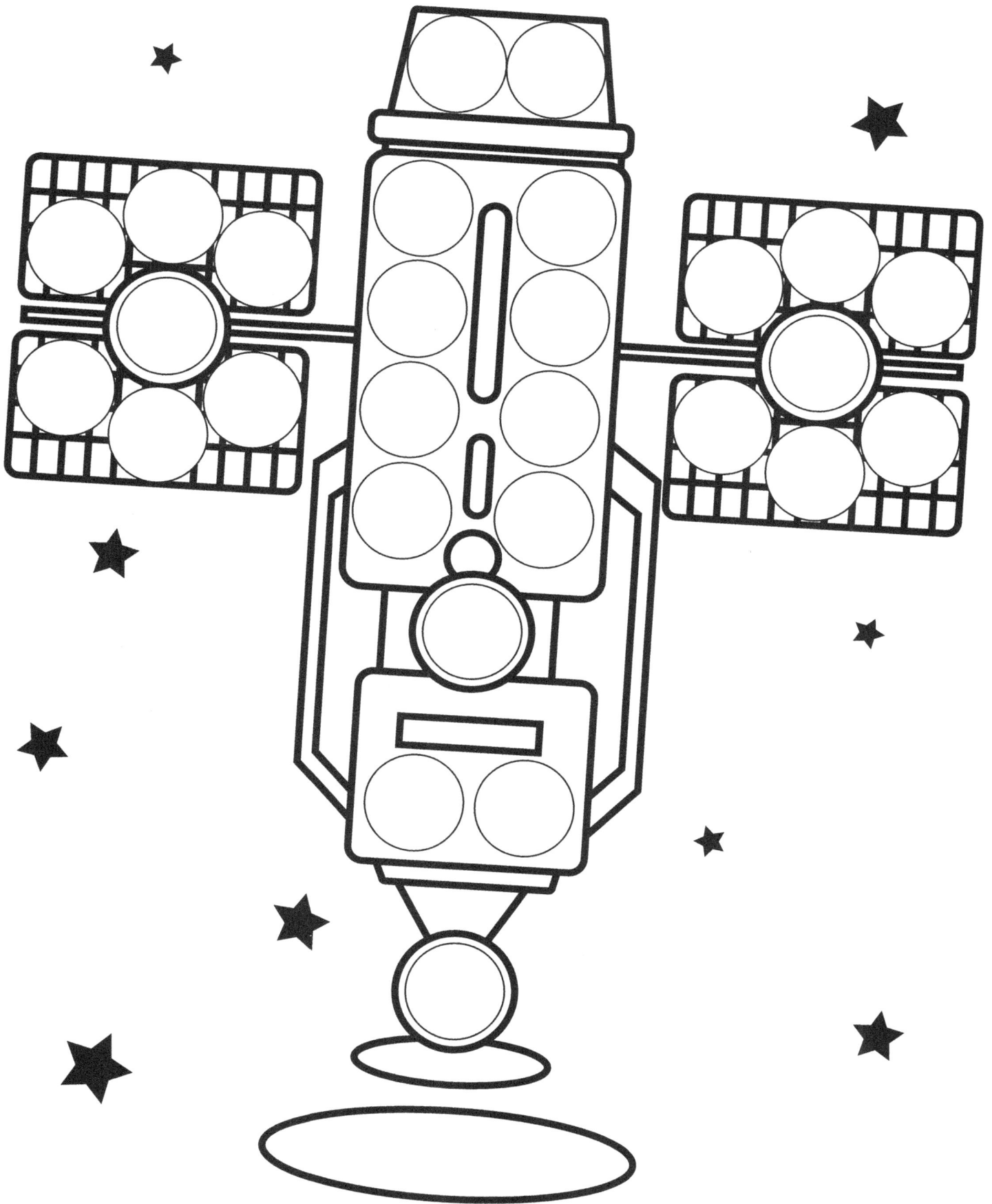

SATELLITE

TOW TRUCK

TRACTOR

TRACTOR

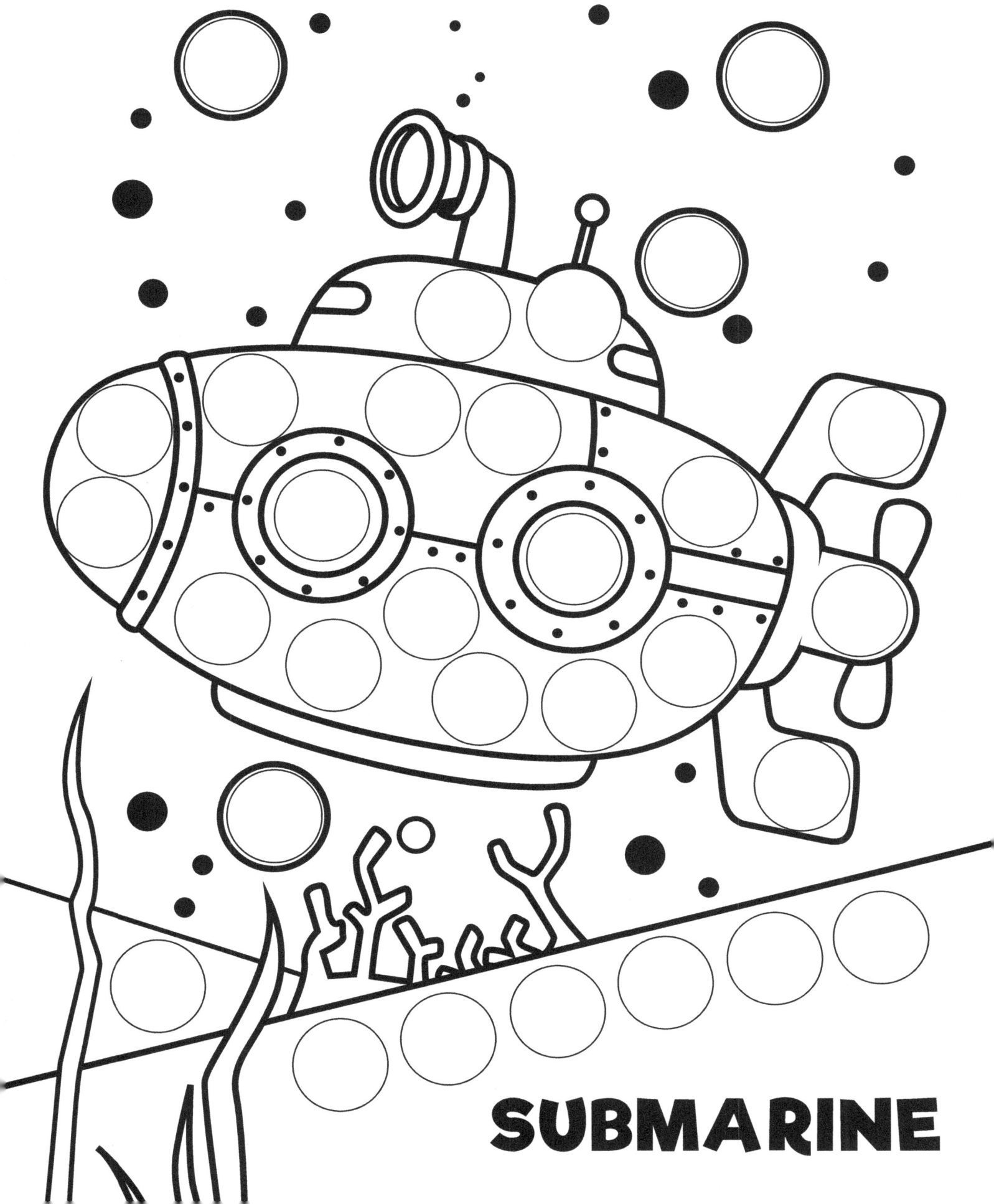

SUBMARINE

WINDSURF

SPACE CAPSULE

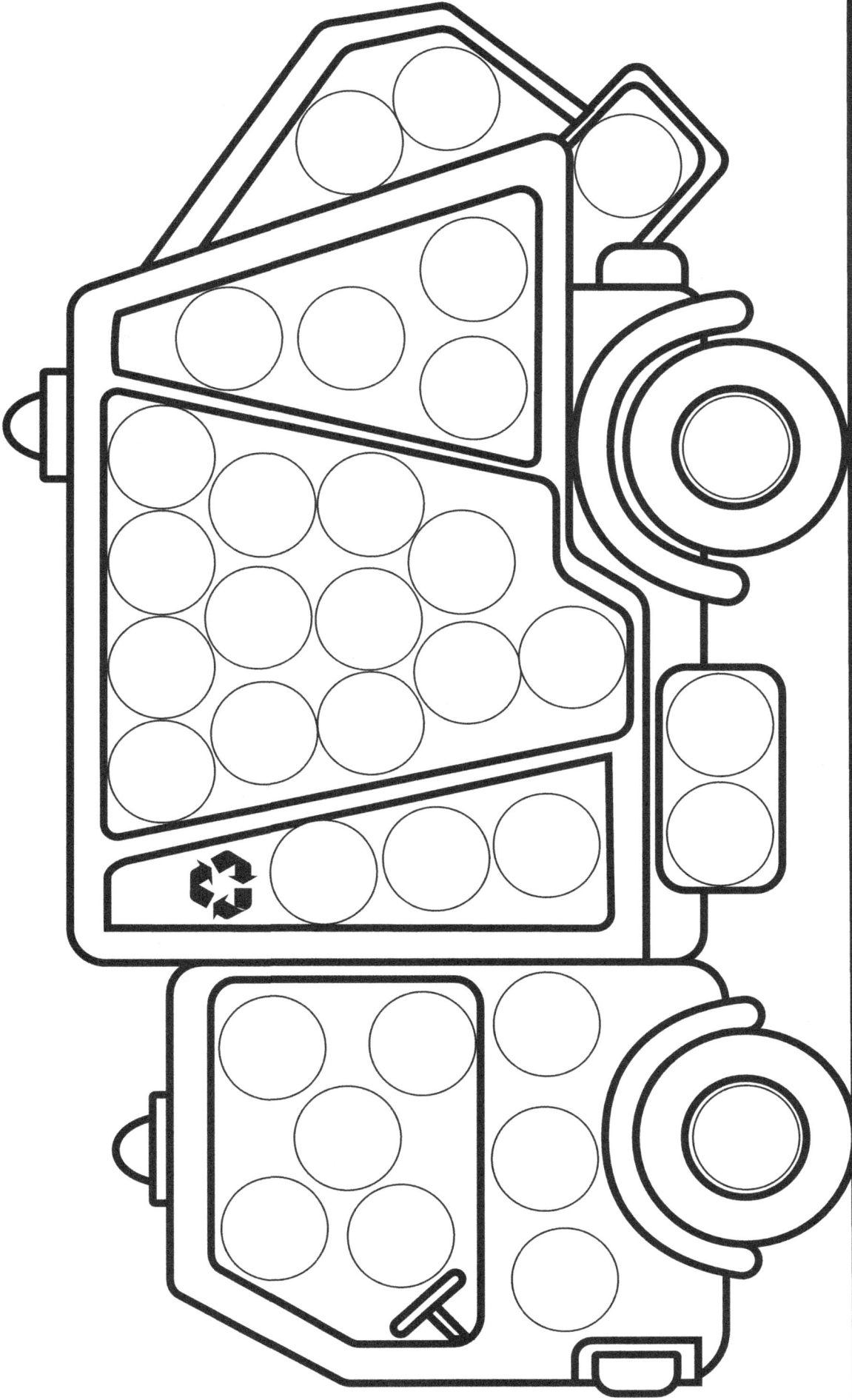

RECYCLING TRUCK

Made in the USA
Las Vegas, NV
21 January 2025